D1053434

BEYOND GLOBAL GOVERNANCE

Prospects for Global Government

James A. Yunker

University Press of America,® Inc.
Lanham · Boulder · New York · Toronto · Plymouth, UK

University Press of America,® Inc.
4501 Forbes Boulevard
Suite 200
Lanham, Maryland 20706
UPA Acquisitions Department (301) 459-3366

10 Thornbury Road
Plymouth PL6 7PP
United Kingdom

Printed in the United States of America
British Library Cataloging in Publication Information Available

Library of Congress Control Number: 2014934368
ISBN: 978-0-7618-6359-5 (clothbound : alk. paper)
eISBN: 978-0-7618-6361-8

™ The paper used in this publication meets the minimum requirements of American National Standard for Information Sciences—Permanence of Paper for Printed Library Materials, ANSI Z39.48-1992

Contents

Preface

The sovereign nation-state system has been the bedrock principle of international relations throughout the last several hundred years of human history. Consolidated in the early modern era, the nation-state system did indeed represent a significant advance over the earlier system of independent empires, kingdoms, principalities, city-states, and assorted tribal groupings. The fewer the independent political entities in the world, the less opportunity for warfare among them. On the other hand, the modern era during which the nation-state has been dominant has also witnessed dazzling progress in all areas of technology, including the technology of weaponry. The effectiveness of modern weaponry has become such that when warfare does break out among nations, despite the best efforts of their respective diplomatic corps, the slaughter and destruction is prodigious and horrific. The relatively recent addition of nuclear weapons to the mix arouses legitimate concern that the next world war might be our last. Apart from concerns over possible nuclear holocaust, the advance of technology has enabled a population explosion throughout the world that is placing increasing pressure upon the limited global resource base. While this threat is not as dramatic as the possibility of instantaneous nuclear disaster, its very long-term consequences might be almost as dire.

The idea of a universal polity embracing the entire territory and population of the Earth has fascinated visionary thinkers for centuries. But it was not until the twentieth century that the idea came into sharp focus. At least three factors played a role. First, two disastrous world wars plus the possibility of an even more disastrous nuclear third world war made people more keenly aware than ever before of the overwhelming destructiveness of modern military weaponry. Second, it was only during the twentieth century that the technologies of communications and transportation advanced to a point to make a global political organization feasible in a practical sense. Finally, the establishment during the century of two international organizations with universalist aspirations, first the League of Nations and then the United Nations, demonstrated the latent desire among a large proportion of the human population for an effective global authority to assist humankind in its continuing efforts toward a higher level of security and prosperity. While neither the League of Nations nor its successor, the United Nations, fulfilled the highest aspirations of their founders, they did accomplish some tangible good, and perhaps even more importantly, they have provided concrete, visible symbols of what might be achieved in the future through the establishment of a legitimate, full-fledged, effective and benign federal world government.

Needless to say, at this point the establishment of such a government still seems a long way off. There is an extremely strong consensus among most people today that while world government is a good idea in theory, it would almost certainly be a disaster in practice. Part of the reason for the continued rejection of the world government possibility is ever-growing confidence—especially since the dramatic abatement of the Cold War in the early 1990s—in "global governance" as a practical means of coping with all the problems of the world. This trend is fostering an unwarranted and dangerous degree of complacency among many people, even historians and political scientists who ought to know better. Some enthusiasts for global governance go so far as to proclaim that there is now absolutely no reason for establishing a world government because any possible good that a world government might accomplish can just as easily be accomplished by the agencies and activities associated with contemporary global governance. Since contemporary global governance is essentially equivalent to global government, they ask, why bother establishing a global government? But if such an equivalence did exist, this question could be turned around: why *not* establish a global government?

The fact is, of course, that contemporary global governance is in no way equivalent to a formally established global government. This is just as clear as the fact that the United Nations is not a global government in any meaningful sense of the term "government." The term "government" implies something well beyond both contemporary global governance, and the United Nations as it is presently constituted. The reason why a global government has not been established in the real world is the continuing apprehension among the large majority of people today that such a government would, at best, become a nightmare of political oppression and bureaucratic strangulation, and at worst, it would soon precipitate a civil war of such monumental proportions as to dwarf anything in the previous experience of humanity.

As a shock reaction to the first use (and so far only use) of nuclear weapons in 1945 to hasten the surrender of Japan at the end of World War II, during the immediate postwar period there developed what can only be described as a "world government boom." During that period, more so than at any other time before or since, the view became quite widespread that a very centralized and authoritarian world government should be immediately established in order to ward off the imminent threat of catastrophic nuclear holocaust. Such a government would encompass every nation in the world, and it would monopolize any and all weapons of mass destruction, including (especially) nuclear weapons. This notion of world government is descriptively designated the "omnipotent world state." The omnipotent world state is, at one and the same time, the ideal of most world federalists and the nightmare of world government opponents.

The world government boom of the immediate postwar period turned out to be an extremely ephemeral phenomenon. The emerging conflict between the Western nations and the Soviet Union, grounded in drastically divergent ideologies, very quickly damped down the enthusiasm for world government. Both sides rejected the possibility of such a government for fear that it might become dominated by the other side. As for the threat of nuclear holocaust, the marvelous flexibility of the human mind soon discounted that. After all, people reasoned, surely no national leader would be "stupid enough" to bring about nuclear war. Despite the dominance of this belief throughout the world, there remains a possibility that this is no more than a sophisticated form of wishful thinking.

In the judgment of this author, it is a mistake to dismiss the possibility of federal world government. While I completely agree with world government skeptics that the omnipotent world state is inadvisable both at the present time and into the foreseeable future, I do not agree that this is the end of the story as far as world government is concerned. I am convinced that there exist practicable designs for a limited federal world government that would go qualitatively beyond the United Nations of today—but not so far as to constitute a serious threat to the legitimate national interests of its member nations. In other words, there exists a happy medium somewhere between the excessively centralized and powerful omnipotent world state of traditional world federalist thinking, and the United Nations of today, which is little more than a poorly funded and little respected international debating society.

It has long been my belief that the establishment of an intelligently designed world government could and would make a major contribution to the successful future development of human civilization. It would be a practical means of furthering the goals of global governance in the true sense. Effective global governance in the absence of effective global government I consider to be a myth—an especially pernicious, dangerous and dysfunctional myth. It is a myth that supports the dominance of an international policy best described as "let's drift and see what happens." There is a distinct possibility that we will eventually drift into disaster—a disaster that would be especially tragic because it was so needless.

Throughout my adult life, it has been my mission to persuade people to open their minds to new possibilities, to "think outside the box"—as the standard cliché puts it. To this end, I have developed a tentative blueprint for a world government for which I propose the name "Federal Union of Democratic Nations." Absolutely fundamental to the Federal Union concept are two reserved rights of the member nations: the right to secession, and the right to maintain independent military forces. To traditional world federalists, these features are completely unacceptable: their incorporation would render the world government totally ineffectual and useless. But without these reserved national rights, there will be no world government, and human civilization will continue to proceed along the perilous path of absolute national sovereignty until—perhaps—disaster strikes. To traditional world federalists, I would have to say that the only world government more ineffectual and useless than the proposed Federal Union of Democratic Nations, is no world government at all. And no world government at all is what we have now, and what we will continue to have into the indefinite and unforeseeable future, unless enough people can be persuaded to open their minds to this innovative approach to world government. There is nothing especially complicated about this new approach, but it does require a certain amount of mental flexibility and vision.

Throughout my career as a professor of economics, I have worked intermittently at developing and communicating the Federal Union idea. On the other hand, my professional work has not revolved entirely around the visionary project of world government. The overall level of skepticism concerning visionary projects in general, and world government in particular, operates as a deterrent to undue concentration on this topic. Thus the great majority of my research and writing in economics and related areas has dealt with conventional issues and problems, some of them tangentially related to the possibility of world government, but most of them not.

Nevertheless, over a prolonged period of time, my published output on the subject of world government has become fairly substantial. My first book-length advocacy of world government was published in 1993: *World Union on the Horizon: The Case for Supernational Federation.* Since then I have published four more books on the subject: *Rethinking*

World Government: A New Approach (2005), *Political Globalization: A New Vision of Federal World Government* (2007), *The Grand Convergence: Economic and Political Aspects of Human Progress* (2010), and *The Idea of World Government: From Ancient Times to the Twenty-First Century* (2011). In conjunction with book work, I have also written a substantial number of essays on world government, which delve into certain aspects of the issue in more detail than can be accommodated within a book. One of the books listed above (*Rethinking World Government: A New Approach*) was in fact a collection of six essays, four of which had been previously published at the time the book appeared. The present volume can be considered a sequel to *Rethinking World Government*: it contains five essays, all of which were written after 2005, three of which have been published in various print journals, one of which was a contribution to an "online conference" on world government and world citizenship, and one of which is previously unpublished.

Although much of the material contained in this book is available elsewhere, I trust that the interested reader will find it convenient to have all these contributions gathered together in one location. In addition, these essays provide what many people might consider a more accessible avenue than any of my books to this innovative approach to the protean topic of world government. All the essays in this volume are stand-alone pieces, each of which provides the reader with a brief but comprehensive account of the Federal Union proposal, along with some discussion, shorter or longer as the case may be, on its pros and cons. Thus any one of the essays will serve as an entry-point to a new way of thinking about world government. Needless to emphasize, the downside of this is that there is a certain amount of repetition to be found within these pages. For a reader intending to plow through every one of these essays, a word of apology is offered in advance on the matter of repetition. But hopefully most readers will understand the reason for the repetition, and will also allow for the fact that when it comes to presenting ideas that will initially be difficult for some people to fully comprehend and appreciate, a certain amount of repetition may be advantageous.

James A. Yunker
Macomb, Illinois
January 2014

Abstracts and Acknowledgments

1. Beyond Global Governance: Prospects for Global Government. Published in *International Journal on World Peace* 26(2): 7-30, June 2009. Reprinted by permission of Professors World Peace Academy.
While it is clear that a world government would considerably reduce the threat of nuclear war, only a very tiny minority of world government advocates believes that this advantage outweighs the countervailing disadvantage that such concentration of political and military power might set the stage for global tyranny. A proposal is put forward for a type of world government that would be far less centralized and powerful than is normally envisioned. Despite its limitations, this plan of world government would make a valuable, albeit gradual and evolutionary, contribution to the furtherance of global governance and the assurance of the future destiny of human civilization.

2. Recent Consideration of World Government in the IR Literature: A Critical Appraisal. Published in *World Futures* 67(6): 409-436, August 2011. Reprinted by permission of Taylor & Francis.
Alexander Wendt's 2003 article "Why a World State Is Inevitable" has generated a certain amount of discussion and controversy regarding world government within the international relations profession. Inasmuch as the question of inevitability is only sensibly considered with reference to existent reality, and as world government is not yet part of existent reality, Wendt's proposition is clearly not meant to be taken literally. Rather it is deliberately provocative: intended merely to elicit additional serious thought about the world government possibility. While it is certainly arguable that additional serious thought about this possibility is

well merited, the published contributions to date have emphasized nebulous theoretical and methodological issues to a far greater extent than the substantive pros and cons of a potential future world government. Thus the recent contributions are of limited usefulness for illuminating the practical question of whether or not an actual world government would advance the human prospect. It is argued that this practical question cannot be sensibly addressed unless in the light of a specific institutional proposal for world government. Along the authority-effectiveness continuum separating the relatively ineffectual existent United Nations on the one hand, and the traditional world federalist ideal of the omnipotent world state on the other, there are intermediate possibilities not subject to the respective disadvantages of the extreme endpoints of this continuum. Evaluations of world government by IR professionals will become more reliable and useful to the extent they focus on these intermediate possibilities.

3. Evolutionary World Government. Published in *Peace Research: The Canadian Journal of Peace and Conflict Studies* 44(1): 95-126, 2012. Reprinted by permission of the publisher.
Development of the concept of "evolutionary socialism" around the turn of the twentieth century had a major impact on political and socioeconomic trends throughout the century. Revisionist thinkers such as Eduard Bernstein abandoned the orthodox Marxist position that socialism must necessarily involve social ownership of the nonhuman factors of production, and that socialism in this pure sense could only be achieved through violent revolution. In so doing, they laid the basis for the later success of social democracy in Western Europe and throughout the world. This paper argues that an analogous concept, "evolutionary world government," might lay the basis for a successful world federalist movement during the twenty-first century. By abandoning the current world federalist ideal of the omnipotent world state, and envisioning as the immediate objective a limited rather than an unlimited world government, a solid foundation might be laid for gradual, evolutionary progress toward the long-run goal of an authoritative and effective, yet democratic and benign, federal world government.

4. From National Sovereignty to Global Government: Is There a Plausible Transition Path? First Virtual Congress (online) on World Citizenship and Democratic Global Governance, 2007.

Many world federalists continue to cling to the ideal notion of an omnipotent world government that emerged during the "world government boom" during the immediate post-World War II years. It is argued here that there is absolutely no plausible transition path, of a peaceful nature, between the world we know today and the omnipotent world government ideal. However, a limited world government is a possibility: a world federation that would allow member nations to withdraw at their own discretion, and to maintain armed forces under their direct control. It is simply not true that such a federation would be—as so many world federalists believe—"useless" against the continuing threat of nuclear world war. Such a federation would provide a foundation on which could be based a gradual, evolutionary trend toward greater trust and cooperation within the international community. Eventually a condition might be reached under which a nuclear world war would be virtually unimaginable. Guidelines are suggested for a more effective world federalist movement in the 21st century.

5. Should the United States Champion World Government?
An increasingly prevalent opinion in policy-making circles is that the United States should utilize its preeminent economic and military strength in the contemporary world to guide a coalition of like-minded major powers toward something along the lines of a global Pax Americana. The pursuit of this course over a prolonged period of future time would most likely produce a very unstable and dangerous world. A superior option would be for the United States to participate in guiding the entire family of nation-states toward a genuine—albeit limited—federal world government. As a political entity, such a world state would represent a quantum leap beyond the United Nations of today, but it would not be so militarily dominant as to constitute a serious threat to the legitimate national interests of its member nations. Establishing a properly designed federal world government would enhance the probability that the entire human race, including the citizens of the United States as well as those of all other nations, will continue to survive and thrive into the distant future.

1

Beyond Global Governance: Prospects for Global Government

Governance without Government

Governance is what governments do. One might suspect this from the similarity of the words, and it is confirmed by reference to any reputable dictionary. Nevertheless, the Commission on Global Governance, in its 1995 Report *Our Global Neighborhood*, proclaimed the following: "Global governance is not global government. No misunderstanding should arise from the similarity of the terms. We are not proposing movement towards world government, for were we to travel in that direction we might find ourselves in an even less democratic world than we have—one more accommodating to power, more hospitable to hegemonic ambition, and more reinforcing of the roles of states and governments rather than of the rights of people."[1]

To the small minority of world federalists, this statement is not only perversely erroneous, but suggestive of nothing less than Orwellian newspeak.[2] However, it clearly expresses the overwhelmingly predominant consensus, throughout the world, among the intelligentsia, the political leadership, and the general public. The great majority of the world population, to the limited extent that they reflect upon the possibility of world government at all, envision such a government as tending inevitably, gradually or quickly as the case may be, to a horrific global tyranny of Hitlerian proportions. As Inis Claude put it: "In terms of Western liberalism, the problem is not to get just any kind of world government—Hitler and Stalin were only the most recent of a long series of leaders who would have been glad to provide that—but to get a system of world order that is compatible with the political ideals of the democratic heritage."[3]

No reasonable person doubts that it would be horrible to live under the harsh dominion of an all-powerful world government controlled by a megalomaniac dictator akin to Hitler or Stalin. But it is also true that no reasonable person doubts that it would be horrible to live in a world blighted by continuous warfare, particularly if one of those wars boils over into a global nuclear holocaust. In the aftermath of a nuclear world war, what would remain of human civilization would probably be lorded over by a host of local tyrants and warlords no more benevolent than were Hitler and Stalin. Avoiding world government, therefore, will not necessarily be effective in avoiding totalitarian tyranny. Indeed, modern history seems to suggest that totalitarian tyranny at the national level is frequently associated with war or the fear of war with other nations.

Modern history also seems to suggest that the sovereign nation-state system possesses a strong propensity toward the generation of hostility, conflict and warfare among nations. Of course, war was not invented by nations, which are relatively recent political innovations. War has been a constant in human affairs throughout all prehistory and history, and may be generated by any two or more politically organized groups, whether they be tribes, villages, city-states, principalities, kingdoms, empires, or nations. But owing to the great size of nations, and the close coordination of massive technical and economic resources which they make possible, the modern era of the nation-state has witnessed a quantum jump in both the comprehensiveness and the destructiveness of warfare. Prior to the disastrous events of 1914 through 1945, a period that encompassed two world wars and was concluded with the atomic bombings of Hiroshima and Nagasaki, it was a relatively commonplace opinion (especially among those not immediately and directly engaged in them) that wars were salutary and beneficial for human society, with effects not unlike those of diet and exercise on the human body. Since 1945, this opinion has mostly been confined to fools and madmen.

The world federalist movement of the twentieth century crested in the few short years that separated the end of the Second World War from the beginning of the Korean War.[4] Shocked by the glimpse provided by the destruction of Hiroshima and Nagasaki of a potential nuclear war of the future, humanity toyed, far more seriously than ever before, with the idea of establishing a universalist government embracing all of the peoples and the nations of the world. Unfortunately, the window of opportunity was quickly closed, the victim of an ideologically fueled strategic conflict between the communist nations of the East and the non-communist nations of the West.[5] Political paralysis was not accompanied by technological paralysis, however, and soon atomic bombs were superseded by far more powerful hydrogen bombs. Similarly, relatively slow aircraft were superseded, as the primary means of delivery, by ballistic missiles. The upshot of this was that as of the 1960s, had a decision been taken by the leadership of any of the nuclear superpowers that war was necessary, it was literally true that within a few hours, hundreds of millions of human beings around the world would have been dead or dying, and much of human civilization would have lain in ruins.

People coped with the nightmarish unreality of the situation by means of comforting thoughts to the effect that a nuclear world war would be so overwhelmingly devastating that only madmen would commence one, and since madmen were unlikely to gain control over a nuclear superpower, nuclear world war was therefore extremely unlikely. This is an illustration of a psychological phenomenon well-known to psychiatrists: denial. When reality is too terrible to contemplate, deny reality. The single most important flaw in the comforting argument described above is that madmen in power is not a necessary condition to start a nuclear war. Such a war could be a consequence of the same sort of miscalculated brinkmanship that sparked both World War I and World War II. And, of course, there is always the possibility of an accident.

A New Opportunity?

Throughout the long and perilous decades of the Cold War, the standard critique of world government normally cited the ideological conflict between East and West as a prime example of the "heterogeneity" within the human race that made the formation of a stable and benign world government an impossibility within the foreseeable future. In his 1967 treatise on international organization, for example, Stephen Goodspeed explained the problem as follows: "If, in some desperate effort to solve the problems dividing the Soviets and the Western world, the United Nations were to be transformed into some form of world government with the General Assembly made a legislature based on the democratic principles of popular representation and majority rule, could it succeed in the absence of a majority possessed of common values, interests and goals? The answer is a categorical 'no' since the struggle between East and West would not dissolve merely because the setting was changed."[6] The "desperate effort" referred to is the proposal of Grenville Clark and Louis Sohn for a strengthened United Nations, put forward in their magisterial and influential—yet ultimately ineffectual tome, *World Peace through World Law*.[7]

The collapse and dissolution of the Soviet Union in 1991 has profoundly affected international relations. No longer is the capitalist economic system and the democratic political system under ideological assault by a nuclear superpower. Relations between the United States and the Russian Federation, while still somewhat stiff and restrained, are amicable enough on the surface, especially in view of what went on before. Stockpiles of strategic nuclear weapons on both sides have been significantly reduced—although they are still at levels such that if they were utilized, they could potentially cripple human civilization, if not annihilate it. But the risk of such utilization in the immediate future is widely assumed to be almost nil. Most pundits concur that the Cold War, if not dead, is at least moribund. This is certainly a positive footing on which to commence the third millennium.

The conclusion of World War I saw the formation of the League of Nations, while the conclusion of World War II saw the formation of the United Nations. There is no need to belabor the limitations and liabilities of both these institutions, nor the fact that they were not world governments according to any reasonable usage of the term "government." Despite this, these institutions were extremely significant in manifesting the deep and abiding aspiration within mankind toward a universalist political entity beyond the national governments. We have now witnessed the final denouement of the third great conflict of the twentieth century: the Cold War between East and West. Just as the resolutions of the first two conflicts led to significant advances toward the ultimate goal of a global government, could not the resolution of the third conflict have led to another advance?

Apparently it did not. One has to recognize that there were important qualitative differences between these earlier historical events and the more recent event. First and foremost, World Wars I and II were hot wars in which millions were killed and wounded. Humanity was given a very emphatic lesson on the disadvantages of warfare. The psychic tensions of the Cold War were oppressive, to be sure, but are hardly to be compared with the tremendous amount of physical pain, death, destruction and sorrow caused by World Wars I and II. The fundamental lesson of these earlier wars was that "war is terrible"; the fundamental lesson of the Cold War, as far as a great many are concerned, is that "now that nuclear weapons have made war intolerably terrible, war will not occur." A second major difference is that World Wars I and II were concluded by military victories which prostrated the defeated nations. The Russian Federation of the early 1990s was hardly comparable to the Germany and Austria of 1918, nor to the Germany and Japan of 1945.

Possibly even more important is that the decades of the Cold War created in humanity far greater consciousness than ever before of the global economic gap, the tremendous gulf which separates the high living standards in the minority of rich nations from the low living standards in the majority of poor nations. This economic gap was a major factor in the geopolitical situation during the Cold War, as both the wealthier capitalist nations and the communist nations endeavored to win over the nonaligned Third World nations to their respective sides of the ideological struggle. According to World Bank statistical data, most of the Third World nations made respectable gains in per capita income during the latter part of the twentieth century, the major exception being the nations of sub-Saharan Africa. On the other hand, economic growth has, on the whole, been stronger in the richest nations, with the consequence that the gap between the richest nations and the poorest nations has been getting wider.

Now that the ideological impediment to world government is declining, the relative importance of the economic impediment is rising. During the Cold War, the noncommunist nations were leery of world government on grounds that it might be subverted by the communist nations and transformed into a tool of communist expansionism. At the same time, the communist nations were leery of world government on grounds that it might be subverted (from their point of view) and transformed into a tool of capitalistic reaction. Now that the Cold War is fading, the rich nations are leery of world government on grounds that it might be controlled by the poor nations and transformed into a tool for the radical transfer of current income from the rich nations to the poor nations (a potential policy which I have elsewhere referred to as "Crude Redistribution"). At the same time, the poor nations are leery of world government on grounds that it might be controlled by the rich nations and transformed into a tool for the reestablishment of colonial-style economic exploitation of the poor nations. The principal obstacle to world government has shifted from the East-West ideological conflict to the North-South economic gap.

"Traditional" World Government Proposals

Back in 1946, an obscure academic by the name of Fremont Rider published an obscure book entitled *The Great Dilemma of World Organization*, in which he proposed a solution to the problem which we would today describe as the global economic gap.[8] Rider himself expressed the problem in terms of the gap between the "civilized" and the "uncivilized" nations. The "civilized" nations of North America, Western Europe and so on (i.e., the rich nations) would never consider participating in a world government with genuine power and authority that was subject to majority rule—and that would hence be controlled by the vast, impoverished populations of the "uncivilized" nations. And yet if world government were to be acceptable to all nations, the principle of apportioning voting weight among the nations would have to possess compelling rationality, plausibility and apparent legitimacy.

Rider's proposed solution was to make the respective voting weights of the nations in the world government legislature proportional to their "educational attainments," in terms of total number of years of education completed by their populations. Since the average educational attainment in the "civilized" nations was high, they would enjoy dominant voting weight in the world legislature. But this would be acceptable to the poor nations as well, since it makes good sense to give more voting weight to individuals with more education. Such individuals would presumably utilize their greater voting weight more wisely and intelligently. Rider envisioned arms races being replaced by "education races" as nations enthusiastically threw their resources into educating their respective populations. Their immediate motivation would be to increase their influence in the world government, but this strategy would also increase their economic prosperity, which is largely determined by the productivity of the citizens, which in turn is largely determined by educational attainment. A highly dubious idea, to be sure, but at least it constituted a sincere effort to deal with a serious problem mostly ignored by other, better known formulators of world government schemes.

Dozens of world government proposals were put forward throughout the course of the twentieth century. Most of them repose in profound obscurity. However, the highly ephemeral post-World War II world government boom generated two proposals which achieved a modest level of general recognition, principally because they were put forward in books published by prestigious university presses. The single edition of Giuseppe Borgese's *Foundations of the World Republic* was published by the University of Chicago Press, while the three editions of Grenville Clark and Louis Sohn's *World Peace through World Law* were all published by Harvard University Press. Borgese's blueprint for a Federal Republic of the World was the product of deliberations by a Committee to Frame a World Constitution, chaired by Robert Hutchins, then Chancellor of the University of Chicago.[9] Grenville Clark and Louis Sohn were highly regarded academic specialists in international law whose blueprint for a "strengthened" United Nations would have effectively transformed that organization into a world government (albeit with authority confined to matters directly affecting the maintenance of peace).

The Borgese and Clark-Sohn proposals are exemplary of the typical twentieth century world government proposal in three critical respects. First, the world legislature follows commendably democratic principles, with the inevitable result that representatives from the relatively poor nations of the world would dominate the voting. According to *World Development Indicators*, a database maintained by the World Bank, the per capita income of the United States for 2005 in current dollars was $43,210. For that year, the *WDI* database provides estimates of per capita income for 179 nations with a combined population of 6,278,014,934 (representing 96.9 percent of the estimated total world population for 2005). Of those 179 nations, 120 (67.04 percent) had per capita income less than $5,000 in current U.S. dollars, and 79.51 percent of the total population of 6,278,014,934 resided in those nations. In light of these fundamental statistical realities, it is quite evident that commendably democratic legislative decision-making in a world government would lead to dominant legislative voting weight in the hands of the poorer nations. For example, without going into the details of the computation, by the Clark-Sohn formula, representatives from nations with per capita income less than $5,000 would account for approximately 75 percent of the total number of representatives in the world legislature (in their case, this world legislature would be the General Assembly in the "strengthened" United Nations). A similar situation would transpire under the Borgese proposal, or indeed under any "typical" world government proposal. Under the typical proposal, dominant legislative voting power would be exercised by representatives from poor nations whose populations would have a strong predisposition toward radical global income redistribution.

The second critical characteristic of the typical twentieth century world government proposal is that membership in the world federation would be universal, permanent and irreversible. Any movement by a member nation toward withdrawing from the world federation would be viewed as treasonous and met by force. Therefore, rich nations unwilling to participate in a radical global income redistribution project undertaken by the world federation would not be able to legally and peacefully leave the federation.

The third critical characteristic is that the member nations would be fully disarmed, and all large-scale military forces and heavy armament would be concentrated under the authority of the world federation. As Clark and Sohn put it: [10]

> The complete disarmament of all the nations (rather than the mere 'reduction' or 'limitation' of armaments) is essential for any solid and lasting peace, this disarmament to be accomplished in a simultaneous and proportionate manner by carefully verified stages and subject to a well-organized system of inspection. It is now generally accepted that disarmament must be universal and enforceable. That it must also be complete is no less necessary, since: (a) in the nuclear age no mere reduction in the new means of mass destruction could be effective to remove fear and tension; and (b) if any substantial national armaments were to re-

> main, even if only ten per cent of the armaments of 1960, it would be impracticable to maintain a sufficiently strong world police force to deal with any possible aggression or revolt against the authority of the world organization. We should face the fact that until there is *complete* disarmament of every nation without exception there can be no assurance of genuine peace.

What this means is that if the world federation were to undertake a radical global income redistribution project, rich nations unwilling to participate in this project and desirous of leaving the federation, would possess no military power with which to support and enforce this desire.

It is important to recognize that a scenario of drastic global income redistribution, entailing the relative impoverishment of the populations of the rich nations to benefit the populations of the poor nations, does not necessarily require a megalomaniac dictator "taking over" the world government by means of a coup d'état. Quite possibly the enabling legislation would be passed by the large majority of a democratically elected legislature, would be implemented and enforced by a democratically elected executive authority, and would be duly reviewed and approved by a democratically accountable judiciary. The effective implementation of the policy in the rich nations might well require considerable force, but this force would be deployed by a world government enjoying the high degree of legitimacy conferred by democratic accountability. Of course, rioting and armed resistance throughout the rich nations would generate "emergency conditions" that would greatly facilitate the advent of a dictator.

The typical post-World War II world government proposal, motivated as it is by the overriding purpose of reducing the threat of nuclear war, is basically oblivious of this problem. The typical world government advocate would respond to objections based on this problem with the assertion that the threat of nuclear holocaust without world government is far greater than the threat of global tyranny with world government, whether this tyranny comes about owing to radical global income redistribution or anything else. The impotence of the world federalist movement throughout the height of the Cold War, at a time when instantaneous nuclear disaster was a far greater danger than it is today, is sufficient testimony to the unpersuasiveness of this assertion.

A New Approach to World Government

It does not require great genius, but only a modicum of mental flexibility, to perceive that there are practical alternatives to the "typical" world government proposal, alternatives which would respond plausibly to the problem outlined, as well as to others of a similar nature. For example, this author's proposal for a Federal Union of Democratic Nations envisions a limited world government very much distinct from the typical world government proposal—yet which would represent an authentic government entity a quantum leap beyond the United Nations of today.[11] The problem with the United Nations is that from its beginning in 1945 as a reconstructed League of Nations with some additional members (most importantly the United States), it was heir to the crippling weaknesses of its predecessor. Although of considerable symbolic significance as a potential steppingstone to a genuine world government, it has mostly been simply a debating society for national ambassadors, with a spotty record of success in its primary mission of preserving peace. Most importantly, the UN had very little effect on the development and course of the Cold War, a period in history during which global human civilization teetered precariously over the abyss of nuclear holocaust. It is high time for humanity to move beyond the UN. In longer historical perspective, the United Nations period might be considered analogous to the Articles of Confederation period in early United States history, before the Articles were superseded by the "more perfect union" embodied in the U.S. Constitution ratified in 1788.

The three critical characteristics enumerated above of the typical world government proposal are as follows: (1) the voting principle in the world government legislature would place dominant voting power in the hands of representatives from poor nations; (2) member nations could not legally and peacefully withdraw from the world federation; (3) member nations could not maintain large-scale military forces and heavy armament under their own control. Three critical characteristics of the alternative world government proposal for a Federal Union of Democratic Nations are respectively as follows: (1) the voting principle in the world government legislature would preclude the passage of any legislation on which the rich nations and the poor nations could not achieve consensus; (2) member nations would have a permanent and inalienable right to withdraw from the Federal Union at any time; (3) member nations would have a permanent and inalienable right to maintain whatever military forces and heavy armament (including nuclear weapons) they desire. Let us look at each of these in turn.

According to the proposed "dual voting" system in the unicameral world legislature (tentatively designated the Union Chamber of Representatives), any proposed measure would have to be passed by a 60 percent majority on two bases: the population basis and the material basis. In the population vote, a representative's voting weight would be equal to the proportion of the population of the entire Union represented by the population of his or her own district. In the material vote, that same representative's voting weight would be equal to the proportion of the overall revenue of the entire Union represented by the revenue raised in that representative's district. With respect to taxation, the proposal envisions the Federal Union's taxing authority confined to a flat percentage, probably somewhere around five percent, of each nation's Gross National Product. The rich nations, as providers of most of the Union's tax revenues, would dominate the material vote and would thereby possess an effective veto power against such unacceptable proposals as drastic global income redistribution. Using World Bank data for 2005, for example, over 75 percent of voting weight in the material vote would be disposed by representatives from nations with per capita income in excess of $20,000. At the same time, the populous poorer nations would dominate the population vote and would thereby possess an effective veto power against proposals that they would regard as unacceptable. Only measures on which both the richer nations and the poorer nations could achieve a reasonable degree of consensus would be capable of passing on both votes.

Note that the practical relevance of the distinction between the population vote and the material vote would be obviated were all nations of the world to have approximately equal per capita income. This condition would be the long-term objective of a massive global economic development program along the lines of the post-World War II Marshall Plan, only on a far larger scale both financially and geographically. Dual voting, and other institutional proposals designed to cope with the North-South economic gap, are intended as a short-run solution to the problem. The long-run solution to the problem would be to eliminate the gap. Of course, conventional opinion holds that the economic gap can only be overcome by the efforts of the poor nations themselves, and that "throwing money at the problem" in the form of large-scale foreign aid is not only futile but probably counter-productive. A somewhat analogous opinion in 1940 would have held that the problem of Nazi aggression could not be solved by "throwing money" into armaments. Of course, one cannot solve the problem of worldwide poverty simply by "throwing money" at it—the money has to be converted into capital goods utilized in productive enterprises. It would not be feasible to enter here into a discussion of the success probability of a massive global economic development program. However, it is likely that this probability is considerably larger than is commonly assumed.[12]

Of course, it would be useless to deny that the outcome of a massive global economic development program *could* in fact be just as conservatives would argue: the proliferation of graft and corruption on a proportionately massive scale, and little or no economic progress in the poor nations. This is where the second critical characteristic of the alternative world government proposal would become relevant: that member nations would have a permanent and inalienable right to withdraw from the Federal Union at any time. Let us imagine that the global economic development program is placing heavy economic burdens on the rich nations, while in the poor nations most of the benefits are going to a small minority of corrupt bureaucrats and dishonest businessmen, with little or no benefit accruing to the general population. The rich nations would then be able to approach the world government with the following proposition: "Either the global economic development program is scaled down drastically or terminated altogether, or we will be forced to depart the federation." Presumably this recommendation of the rich nations would be speedily implemented. If not, the world federation would in all probability dissolve completely, since a federation composed entirely of the poor nations probably would not be able to accomplish much. If that happens, humanity would be back to where we are today, sadder but wiser, but otherwise none the worse for wear.

But what about the possibility that the world government would utilize its military power to crush any opposition to its policies, be they a massive global economic development program or anything else? This is where the third critical characteristic of the alternative world government proposal would become relevant: member nations would have a permanent and inalienable right to maintain whatever military forces and heavy armament (including nuclear weapons) they desire. The rich nations, for example, would by no means be defenseless against a world government determined to pursue a massive global economic development program even though the futility of the program was becoming obvious to the rich nations. In this new view of world government, general disarmament is not viewed as a short-term objective to be accomplished immediately upon the formation of the world government. It is viewed rather as a long-term goal which would probably not be accomplished for many decades. In this new view, the world government is not the end of political evolution, but rather a part of political evolution. The existence and operation of the world government would slowly but steadily enhance that spirit of cosmopolitan toleration which facilitates international cooperation and coordination. If the world government develops as hoped, member nations would gradually feel more and more secure, and would correspondingly—and voluntarily—reduce their military spending and their arms stockpiles.

The Chicken or the Egg?

Which came first—the chicken or the egg? What makes the question absurd, and therefore humorous, is that neither the modern chicken nor the modern egg came first. The modern chicken-egg-chicken progression is the result of millions of years of evolutionary development with roots in the primeval slime. Those who argue that it is necessary to have a high level of global homogeneity prior to having an effective world state are equivalent to those who would argue, in response to the chicken-egg question, that since chickens come out of eggs, then the egg came first. The problem with this argument, obviously, is that it is also true that eggs come out of chickens.

If we take social and attitudinal homogeneity to be the egg, and the effectiveness of state organization to be the chicken, the relevance of the chicken-egg question becomes clear. A population which is politically united within the same state organization tends to become, over time, more socially and attitudinally homogeneous. Similarly, as a given population becomes more socially and attitudinally homogeneous, its state organization tends to become more effective (among other reasons, because it expends less resources on enforcing the majority will upon recalcitrant minorities). There is a progressive, interactive, mutually reinforcing, snowballing process between the social and attitudinal homogeneity of a given population, and the effectiveness of the state organization in which it is politically united.

It is reasonably obvious, to all but the most enthusiastic (and unrealistic) proponents of world government, that the degree of homogeneity among nations today is insufficient to support a world state with an amount of practical and moral authority over the nations of the world analogous, for example, to that of the national government of the United States today over the 50 state governments. This means that an *extremely* powerful, effective and authoritative world state is an impossibility at the present time. It does not mean that a *somewhat* powerful, effective and authoritative world state is an impossibility at the present time. The constraints which are integral components of my own proposal for a Federal Union of Democratic Nations would make this limited form of world government acceptable to many if not most nations of the world today—if and when they become aware of the proposal. If and when such a world government is established, it would then commence a long-term process of gradual evolution toward a higher level of homogeneity among its citizens, and a higher level of effectiveness in its operations.

It is not essential that the world government, in its early stages, be active and powerful. Rather it is essential only that it exists and is visible.

The world government should have an attractive flag and eye-catching emblems, an appealing anthem, a capital city which would become a major tourist destination because of its many attractions (museums, Disneyworld-type theme parks, and so on). These are hardly frivolous and unimportant matters. They would be critical to the development of what might be termed "supernational patriotism." Human beings are moved by just such tangible symbols to a far greater extent than they are by abstract concepts and principles, no matter how high-minded and commendable these concepts and principles may be.

Many well-intentioned individuals today (such as the members of the Commission on Global Governance, an excerpt from whose *Report* commenced this article) urge that all humanity develop a sense of global community, of brotherhood transcending national boundaries and embracing the entire human family from Manhattan sophisticates to rain forest tribespeople. But "global community" and similar terms denote merely abstract concepts. Most individuals preaching these concepts today have not yet perceived that a properly designed federal world government, as a tangible symbol, could indeed make a major contribution to the attitudinal development which they espouse—without degenerating into a totalitarian nightmare comparable to what was brought about in the twentieth century by Adolf Hitler and Joseph Stalin. Proper safeguards are capable of reducing the probability of a totalitarian outcome to an acceptably low level. But with these safeguards in place, a functioning world government, by virtue merely of its existence, would provide potent assistance to the further development of the cosmopolitan attitudes advocated by the great majority of educated, enlightened people today.

A Stable and Benign "New World Order"?

Few people doubt that the world is currently a much safer place than it was twenty-five years ago. The abandonment of Marxist ideology by the components and satellites of the ex-Soviet Union has greatly eased tensions. Around the world, military spending and arms stockpiles have been reduced. The danger of instantaneous nuclear holocaust has been reduced to a level that many consider negligible and insignificant. The downside of these developments, as far as the future destiny of the human race is concerned, is the loss of a sense of urgency, the growth of complacency, and the dominance of a policy best described as "let's drift and see what happens." Not even the traumatic events of September 11, 2001, have apparently dislodged humanity's strong consensus that the current international status quo situation is—if not the best of all *imagi-*

nable worlds—at least the best of all *possible* worlds.

During the Cold War, it was routinely asserted that world government was no longer necessary to alleviate the threat of nuclear world war, because nuclear weapons had made such a war so immensely destructive that the rationality of mankind would forever preclude one from happening. Now that the Cold War is over, it is routinely asserted that world government is even more unnecessary because voluntary cooperation among the nations will accomplish anything worthwhile that a world government would have accomplished. In other words, informal "global governance" is just as efficacious as formal "global government."[13] Advocates of world government are typically dismissed as "utopian dreamers." What may in fact be a "utopian dream" is that the development of cosmopolitan tolerance and mutual respect among sovereign and independent nations, subject to no higher political authority than themselves, will forever spare human civilization from a nuclear war for which the weapons are ready and waiting. World government skeptics allege that humanity is not sufficiently rational to establish a world government. On what basis, therefore, do these skeptics also allege that humanity *is* sufficiently rational to forever avoid nuclear war?

Even if we make the seemingly reasonable assumption that national governments today are basically rational and will not engage deliberately in actions likely to precipitate warfare, we are still confronted by the fact that history has sometimes been fundamentally altered by irresponsible non-state actors of dubious rationality. The irrational actions of these non-state actors sometimes compel state actors to take actions they would not otherwise contemplate. Consider the fact, for example, that the spark that ignited World War I was the assassination, in the city of Sarajevo on June 28, 1914, of the Austrian Archduke Franz Ferdinand and his wife by the teenaged Serbian nationalist Gavrilo Prinzip, a member of the Young Bosnia society that was supplied with weapons by the Black Hand terrorist organization. Although some elements of the Serbian military provided surreptitious training and support for the Black Hand, it is very unlikely that the highest officials of the Serbian government authorized and planned the assassination of Franz Ferdinand. Nevertheless, the natural suspicions of the Austrian government to this effect led to the ultimatum that, within a month, launched the "Great War" or "War to End All Wars."

There are obvious parallels between such past terrorist organizations as the Black Hand and contemporary terrorist organizations such as Al-Qaeda. The latter dramatically demonstrated its capabilities on September 11, 2001, when it destroyed the World Trade Center and killed thousands of people. Had circumstances been different, specifically if the

Soviet Union had still existed on that date, and had it considered it a sacred duty to oppose the invasion of Afghanistan by the United States (a "capitalist imperialist power" according to traditional communist ideology)—then there might well have occurred a march to war in 2001 very similar to the 1914 march to war following the assassination of Franz Ferdinand. A functioning world government making significant progress against the global inequality problem would reduce the incidence of terrorist attacks, and more importantly it would reduce the probability that such attacks, when they occur, will lead to international warfare.

That the collapse and dissolution of the Soviet Union has generated a new world order is obvious. The salient question is whether this new world order will be stable and benign—or otherwise. There are warning signs, for those who have eyes to see them. In the United States, for example, unquestionably the greatest single military power in the world today, there are right-wing extremist groups who interpret the "new world order" as a giant conspiracy to enslave the United States.[14] These groups think it would be a sensible policy for the United States to "nuke" anyone or anything that represents a serious threat to U.S. national interests—and they see serious threats everywhere. Can these groups be kept under control forever? Would it be possible to keep them under control, for example, if an international terrorist organization manages to detonate a nuclear device in a major U.S. city? That certain terrorist organizations would happily carry out such an action—were they in possession of a nuclear device—was incontrovertibly established by the horrific events of September 11, 2001.

Meanwhile, there is unease in the rest of the world over what many perceive as unrestrained U.S. power. The "balance of power," on which all hopes for peace have hitherto depended in the modern era of national sovereignty—is now out of balance. Not everyone perceived in the 1991 Gulf War, for example, a heartening example of international solidarity against aggression by a nation under the control of a mini-Hitler. Some saw it as an ominous portent of global hegemony by the United States alone, or by an alliance among the small minority of wealthy nations.[15] According to this view, the United States and its allies would never have bothered if the victim of the aggression, Kuwait, had not happened to be a major oil exporter. The main point of the exercise was not (in this view) to teach a lesson to would-be aggressors in the future, but to keep the price of oil low. Those who thought this way were also of the opinion that it was important that "counterweights" be built up against the power of the United States.

The 2003 invasion of Iraq by a "coalition" consisting almost entirely of the United States and (to a much lesser extent) Britain, generated a wave of protest not only in the Middle East but throughout the world. While few of the protesters would have denied that Saddam Hussein had degenerated into a vicious tyrant, and that he represented a "threat to stability" in the Middle East, they doubted that his regime presented such a clear and present danger to the security of the United States and its allies as to justify military invasion. The quick military victory of U.S. and U.K. forces in Iraq intensified apprehensions throughout the rest of the world that the United States, aided and abetted by a handful of its closest allies, was evolving into an international bully that would in future take upon itself the task of preemptively eliminating, via military conquest, all real and perceived threats to its national interests. No doubt those concerned that the United States might evolve into an international bully are deriving considerable comfort from the fact that postwar Iraq has become a quagmire that is swallowing up substantial U.S. human and material resources. The United States may be the only "nuclear superpower" in the world today, but there are several other "nuclear powers"—most notably the Russian Federation—that will eventually confront the U.S. should it become unduly aggressive. This is not a healthy basis for future development.

In Number 6 of *The Federalist Papers*, Alexander Hamilton, in response to the argument that there was no need for a closer political union among the thirteen original states because there was no foreseeable basis for future conflicts among them, wrote as follows: "A man must be far gone in Utopian speculation who can seriously doubt that, if these states should either be wholly disunited, or only united in partial confederacies, the subdivisions into which they might be thrown would have frequent and violent contests with each other. To presume a want of motives for such contests as an argument against their existence, would be to forget that men are ambitious, vindictive, and rapacious. To look for a continuation of harmony between a number of independent, unconnected sovereignties in the same neighborhood, would be to disregard the uniform course of human events, and to set at defiance the accumulated experience of the ages." As the title of the Report of the Commission on Global Governance suggests, the world is now a "global neighborhood"—albeit an anarchic and unsettled neighborhood. Hamilton's 1787 argument concerning the original thirteen states is therefore plausibly extrapolated to the nations of the world today.

The opportunities that we possess today to move forward toward a global political unity are unparalleled in history. Continuing technological progress in transportation and communications have rendered the coordination problems of state entities in earlier eras effectively null and void. International commerce and investment, for the first time in history, have risen to such levels as to justify the term "world economy." In fact, the interconnectedness of the global economic system has proceeded to such a high level that problems such as the current worldwide recession (the "global meltdown") could certainly be confronted more effectively if there were a global political authority in existence that would facilitate coordinated anticyclical policy throughout the world. Although the European Union is still a long way from being a meaningful government in the political sense, its strong economic growth since its inception in 1951 with the European Steel and Coal Community demonstrates the potential power of international economic coordination and cooperation. It is especially significant that several of the leading EU member nations of today were engaged in the desperate struggle of World War II only a few years prior to the formation of the ESCC—this manifests the innate ability within humanity to transcend the past when given the incentive and opportunity to do so.

Especially now that the most controversial elements of Marxist ideology are in abeyance, there exists a remarkably high consensus, throughout the world, on some key and critical components of "the good and just society." With Hollywood and Coca Cola Inc. in the vanguard, cultural globalization is proceeding ever onward and upward. Although "Muslim extremism" has been much on peoples' minds since the foundation of Israel in 1948 inflamed the Middle East, the fact remains that all the great religions of the world, including Islam, are basically in favor of universal toleration, compassion, cooperation—attitudes that are fully compatible with a properly designed, democratic, benevolent world government.

But at the same time, there are very serious problems, even leaving aside the persistence of large stockpiles of operational nuclear weapons: most significantly, the interrelated problems of runaway population growth and environmental degradation. A world government might greatly assist and facilitate humanity's efforts to ameliorate these kinds of problems, which if not adequately checked could lead eventually to the downfall of human civilization. If we hesitate too long before taking decisive action, the opportunities we possess today may fade away, setting us irretrievably on the path to disaster.

It is sometimes suggested that it would not matter how rational and reasonable a case might be made for world government—such a government will remain forever impossible because of the immutability of nationalistic pride and prejudice. Any reasonable proposal for world government, at a minimum, addresses the issue of nationalism by specifying a federal form of government in which the member nations would maintain their identities, their governments, their cultures, and a substantial degree of autonomy and sovereignty. Careful consideration of the role of nationalism in history reveals that it is largely associated with the perception of the nation-state as the principal line of defense against subjugation by external forces. But a major purpose of world government would be to alleviate this fear of subjugation.

One variation on the general argument that nations will never allow themselves to be incorporated into a superior political entity is that national leaders will never permit such incorporation as it would diminish their personal authority and prestige. But national leaders—just as all others—are motivated, to a large extent, by the desire for admiration and approbation. Simply put, they want to be remembered favorably in future history books. An opportunity now exists for bold and perceptive national leaders around the world to make a contribution beyond anything they might previously have imagined. As the "founding fathers" of a world union, they would in all probability be highly regarded by future historians.

Notes

1. *Our Global Neighborhood: The Report of the Commission on Global Governance* (New York: Oxford University Press, 1995), p. xvi. The term "global governance" has come into its own in the post-Cold War period. A relatively new scholarly journal utilizes the term as its title, and the term has proliferated in the titles of professional books on international relations and international organization. Two typical examples include Albert J. Paolini, Anthony P. Jarvis, Christian Reus-Smit, eds., *Between Sovereignty and Global Governance: The United Nations, the State and Civil Society* (New York: St. Martin's Press, 1998); Martin Hewson and Timothy J. Sinclair, eds., *Approaches to Global Governance Theory* (Albany, NY: State University of New York Press, 1999).

2. For a variety of trenchant critiques of *Our Global Neighborhood* from the world federalist standpoint, see Errol E. Harris and James A. Yunker, eds., *Toward Genuine Global Governance: Critical Reactions to "Our Global Neighborhood"* (Westport, Ct.: Praeger, 1999).

3. Inis Claude, *Swords into Plowshares: The Problems and Progress of International Organization*, fourth edition (New York: Random House, 1971), p. 430.

4. See the account of this period in Derek Heater, *World Citizenship and Government: Cosmopolitan Ideas in the History of Western Political Thought* (New York: St. Martin's Press, 1996), Chapter 6.

5. The ultimate postwar verdict on world government might be summarized as "very interesting in theory, but extremely unpromising in practice." A major contribution to the enunciation of this verdict was Gerard J. Mangone, *The Idea*

and Practice of World Government (New York: Columbia University Press, 1951).

6. Stephen S. Goodspeed, *The Nature and Function of International Organization*, second edition (New York: Oxford University Press, 1967), p. 663.

7. Grenville Clark and Louis B. Sohn, *World Peace through World Law: Two Alternative Plans*, 3rd enlarged edition (Cambridge, Ma.: Harvard University Press, 1967).

8. Fremont Rider, *The Great Dilemma of World Organization* (New York: Reynal and Hitchcock, 1946).

9. Giuseppe Borgese, *Foundations of the World Republic* (Chicago: University of Chicago Press, 1953).

10. Clark and Sohn, *op. cit.*, p. xv.

11. James A. Yunker, *Political Globalization: A New Vision of Federal World Government* (Lanham, MD: University Press of America, 2007), and *Rethinking World Government: A New Approach* (same publisher, 2005). See also Yunker, "A Pragmatic Route to Genuine Global Governance," in Errol E. Harris and James A. Yunker, eds., *Toward Genuine Global Governance: Critical Reactions to "Our Global Neighborhood"* (Westport, CT.: Praeger, 1999).

12. For a detailed technical argument to this effect, based on computer simulations of a global economic development model, see James A. Yunker, *Common Progress: The Case for a World Economic Equalization Program* (Westport, Ct.: Praeger, 2000). A revised and updated version of this work is available in my article "Could a Global Marshall Plan Be Successful? An Investigation Using the WEEP Simulation Model," *World Development* 32(7): 1109-1137, July 2004. This article was reprinted as Chapter 3 of *Rethinking World Government* (2005).

13. I argue elsewhere that this proposition is merely a comforting myth. See "Effective Global Governance without Effective Global Government: A Contemporary Myth," *World Futures* 67(7): 503-553, October-November 2004. Reprinted as Chapter 5 of *Rethinking World Government* (2005).

14. For a sobering experience of this type of thinking, see Gary H. Kah, *En Route to Global Occupation* (Lafayette, La.: Huntington House Publishers, 1992), which contains such passages as the following (p. 148): "Sovereign nations would cease to exist. A single global economic system would be established and anything left from the old order of things would be purely superficial, such as languages, cultures, names of countries, etc. Any real authority would now rest with an international body controlled by Satan himself."

15. This is the general tenor, for example, in Danilo Zolo, *Cosmopolis: Prospects for World Government* (Cambridge, UK: Polity Press, 1997).

2

Recent Consideration of World Government in the IR Literature: A Critical Appraisal

Introduction

In 2003, Alexander Wendt, the prominent international relations authority, published a paper entitled "Why a World State Is Inevitable" in the *European Journal of International Relations*. In view of the very strong consensus against world government among contemporary international relations professionals, the title is clearly provocative, if not virtually inflammatory. Although it can sensibly be argued that anything that is part of existent human reality was inevitable in a strict sense on the principle of causation, given our limited powers of observation and understanding, it is impossible for anyone to predict with absolute certainty that anything that is not yet part of existent human reality, will come to pass in the future. Specific future events are indeed inevitable according to the principle of causation, but we do not know for sure which specific events will actually occur. In fact, a coldly objective evaluation of the facts we have at hand today suggests that the extinction of the human race within a relatively brief period of geological time, through nuclear war, environmental breakdown, or perhaps both, is at least as likely as the formation of a world state.

Professor Wendt is of course well aware of this; thus the title of his paper is deliberately provocative, and not meant as a definite prediction. Rather it is designed to elicit additional serious thinking within the IR profession about world government. Wendt's inevitability essay has indeed been cited in a number of contributions, but whether this attention will lead to a serious challenge to the existing strong consensus against world government remains to be seen. While most of the contributions seem at least somewhat sympathetic toward world government, none of them significantly amplifies or expands Wendt's argument. In fact, thus far the only full-scale engagement with Wendt's "inevitability thesis" has been critical: Shannon (2005), Wendt (2005).

Some of the citations fall into the "see also" category. One author points out the lack of immediate relevance of the thesis: "Wendt is in a very small minority, and as he puts off the creation of world government for at least another century, see id at 492, the possibility has no relevant short-term implications even if he is correct" (Posner, 2006: 489); while another suggests that there is nothing especially innovative about the thesis: "From time to time a contemporary international relations theorist, like Alexander Wendt, suggests that 'a world state is inevitable' (Wendt 2003, 2005; Shannon 2005), or Daniel Deudney (2006) wishes one were because war has become too dangerous" (Weiss, 2009: 261). If indeed the inevitability thesis is eventually recognized as a serious challenge to the mainstream consensus against world government, quite possibly the outcome will simply be a further refining and strengthening of the conventional "case against world government" that underpins the current consensus.

I will argue here that the current consideration of world government in the IR literature is significantly off-target, and that both the "case for world government" and the "case against world government," as currently perceived, are seriously incomplete and deficient. This is because the world state alternative to the existing international status quo is typically envisioned in terms of the traditional world federalist ideal, referred to here as the "omnipotent world state." As this designation suggests, the omnipotent world state would exercise an effective monopoly on large-scale military forces armed with weapons of mass destruction (including nuclear), it would require the adherence of all nations in the world without exception, and it would be prepared to suppress wars within or between component nations, as well as any challenges to its own authority, with overwhelming armed force. If this is the one and only vision of world government entertained, then the "case against world government" becomes compelling to all but a handful of individuals who are (in the view of the large majority) unduly anxious about the possibility of nuclear world war and/or environmental breakdown. The fact is, however, that there are plausible alternatives that envision a supernational political organization somewhere between the existing United Nations, located at one end of the authority-effectiveness spectrum, and the omnipotent world state, located at the other end. If proper account is taken of these intermediate possibilities, then the "case for world government" is significantly strengthened.

This paper is organized as follows. First, we examine IR theory as it relates to world government. Thus far the consideration of world government in the IR literature has been largely conducted on the basis of very general principles derived from competing theories of realism and constructivism, with very little reference to the institutional specifics and policy directions of such a government. But whether or not a world government is desirable, or even possible, depends critically on its institutions and policies. The theories of realism and constructivism, in and of themselves, are not sufficiently precise in their implications to yield reliable illumination on the world government possibility, so long as that possibility is either left completely undefined, or is confined to the omnipotent world state.

We then examine the specifics of Wendt's teleological argument in light of reactions to it in the IR literature. It is argued that the main points of the debate thus far relate only very weakly to the core questions involved in arriving at a judgment on whether or not a world government would advance the human prospect. It is further argued that little illumination on these core questions is likely to be forthcoming so long as our thinking continues to be organized around only two mutually exclusive alternatives: (1) the status quo, versus (2) the traditional world federalist ideal, descriptively characterized here as the "omnipotent world state." The status quo consists of the efforts of the United Nations and other existing international organizations toward fostering peaceful coexistence and cooperative behavior among the nations of the world. The omnipotent world state, on the other hand, would be a highly centralized and authoritative world government that would stand in relation to the component nations much as the national government of the United States stands in relation to the 50 states. Clearly, with such a strong global authority in existence, peaceful coexistence and cooperative behavior among the nations could be reliably enforced. Nevertheless, if the omnipotent world state were the *only* alternative to the status quo, then no matter what the shortcomings of the status quo, a world state would quite likely, in the view of most, be a "cure worse than the disease."

The following section focuses on a specific plausible alternative to both the status quo and the omnipotent world state. The status quo and the omnipotent world state are two extreme ends of the spectrum of possibilities. A proposal is advanced herein for a federal world government whose power, influence and authority would lie somewhere between that of the existing United Nations and that of the omnipotent world state. If the debate over world government were to focus on an intermediate possibility such as this, it would likely become more fruitful.

The concluding section surveys attitudes on world government within the IR profession as they have evolved over the recent past. While the overall effectiveness of global governance has clearly improved in the two decades since the end of the Cold War, it still falls well short of the imaginable ideal. This elicits the question whether optimally effective global governance needs to be supported by an existent, operational global government. While an existent, operational world government in the image of the traditional world federalist ideal of the omnipotent world state is almost certainly both impractical and inadvisable, there exist less powerful and centralized possibilities that might significantly increase the effectiveness of global governance without running an undue risk of a totalitarian outcome. Serious study of these possibilities is merited.

IR Theory and World Government

The realist theory of international relations posits that nations pursue their own interests within an essentially anarchic international regime, i.e., a regime in which nations are subject to no effective higher authority than themselves. Prominent authorities in the post-World War II realist tradition include Kenneth Waltz (1959, 1979, 2008), Martin Wight (1978), Reinhold Niebuhr (1977), Hedley Bull (1977), and John H. Herz (1976). Constructivist theory posits that nations are similar to individuals in possessing natural tendencies toward cooperative and mutually supportive behavior. Prominent authorities in the more recent, post-Cold War constructivist tradition include Alexander Wendt (1992, 1999), Martha Finnemore (1996), Peter J. Katzenstein (1996), and Rodney Bruce Hall (1999). Both traditions can point to a massive amount of historical evidence that seems supportive. Every aggressive war, broken treaty and forsaken alliance can be cited in support of realism. Meanwhile, every instance of peaceful interaction among nations, from economic trade to (unbroken) treaties to cultural exchanges, can be cited in support of constructivism. Although the realist theory of international relations is generally associated with a somewhat pessimistic attitude about human nature and conservative, hawkish policy preferences, while the constructivist theory is generally associated with a more optimistic attitude about human nature and progressive, dovish policy preferences, the fact remains that there is nothing in the core tenets of either theory that necessarily mandates a particular preference on any particular foreign policy issue.

Prior to the disastrous warfare of the twentieth century, capped by the use of the newly invented atomic bomb on the Japanese cities of Hiroshima and Nagasaki, it was a fairly widespread viewpoint, especially among statesmen and military leaders, that warfare was a permanent constant in international relations—but not an altogether dysfunctional constant. Warfare (in this view) had beneficial effects on human society, somewhat akin to the beneficial effects of diet and exercise on the human body. Warfare was indeed a natural component of Darwinian natural selection, which applies to the struggle for survival among nations no less than it does to the struggle for survival among species.

In the nuclear age, of course, this comfortable attitude toward warfare is no longer prevalent. It is no longer held by even the most hard-nosed and hawkish realists. Indeed, the optimistic view of post-World War II realism, in its various strands (liberal realism, neoclassical realism, and so on), is that an unrestricted nuclear war is highly unlikely precisely because it would be so tremendously destructive. Nations pursue their own self-interests, and a nuclear world war would be in no nation's self-interest. Meanwhile, the constructivists are also fairly optimistic about the matter, because in their view the cautious attitude of contemporary nations toward unrestricted nuclear war is not merely a function of their own crass self-interest; it is also a function of increasingly cosmopolitan attitudes among the citizens and leaders of the various nations. In other words, there is an ongoing socialization process among the nations that is making them more and more predisposed toward peaceful coexistence and mutual cooperation as a general principle.

One is reminded of the Freudian distinction between id, ego and super-ego. A human infant has no regard whatsoever for the interests of others: his or her behavior is guided entirely by a quest for immediate gratification of basic needs (id-directed behavior). As a human person grows and develops, parental or other socialization is applied, involving rewards and punishments, and he or she gradually learns that a sensible and successful pursuit of self-interest requires attention to the interests of others. By early to mid- childhood, the average person is abiding by the various rules and regulations of social life because that course of action will lead to maximum benefit for himself or herself in the long run (ego-directed behavior). This good behavior is driven by self-interest. However, as the person fully matures, it is hypothesized that the rules and regulations become internalized to such an extent that the person follows them even though, in some cases, this is probably *not* in even the person's *long-term* self-interest (super-ego-directed behavior). It is uncertain whether human beings actually make the transition from ego-directed to super-ego-directed behavior. Even cases of what seems to be extraordinarily altruistic behavior, such as that of Mother Teresa, might be explained in terms of self-interest: Mother Teresa may have simply been pursuing the self-interested goal of eternal salvation.

If the behavior of nations were truly id-directed, we imagine that the international regime would be something akin to the Hobbesian state of nature: continual devastating warfare. But just as growing children are soon weaned away from id-directed behavior by the process of socialization, so too nations make the transition to ego-directed behavior, even though they are not functioning under the equivalent of parental or other higher authority. Nations learn from hard experience that if they are too aggressive in the pursuit of their national interests, this will likely provoke armed retaliation by other nations. In other words, while in the international environment there is no formal higher authority over nations, similar to parents, teachers and other authority figures in the development of children into adults, there is an equivalent informal higher authority implicit in the existence of numerous other nations actively pursuing their own interests. But is the relatively peaceful and cooperative behavior of nations (much if not most of the time) to be considered, as the realists would have it, primarily ego-directed? Or is it rather to be considered, as the constructivists would have it, primarily super-ego-directed? I would suggest that this question is both unanswerable and basically unimportant, and thus debates about it are more or less unproductive. What is important is the nature and level of cooperation and mutual support among nations, not its source.

For most people, intuition would probably suggest that to the extent that the constructivist view is closer to the truth than the realist view (that is, nations' behaviors are super-ego-directed to a greater extent than ego-directed), there will be "more" cooperation and mutual support among nations. But how to determine the meaning of "more" in this context? What would be the basis for comparison? Furthermore, for any given policy preference, how do we know the actual motivation underlying that particular policy preference? For example, as a rule U.S. constructivists would be more likely than U.S. realists to support U.S. participation in the International Criminal Court. But this may not indicate a fundamental difference with the realists in their perception of international relations. It could simply be that U.S. constructivists believe that participation in the ICC is more likely be in the best long-term interests of the United States. In other words, there might not be a fundamental difference in terms of U.S. constructivists actually valuing the interests of other nations more equally with the interests of their own nation. Rather it could simply be a matter of applying enlightened national self-interest in preference to unenlightened national self-interest (albeit realists would disagree as to what is and what is not "enlightened" in regard to specific foreign policy issues).

Participation in a world state, of course, would be a far more momentous undertaking than participation in the International Criminal Court. We expect that constructivists would be more receptive to such participation than realists. In "Why a World State is Inevitable," Alexander Wendt, a leading constructivist, states (2003: 529): "Although this question [the question whether a world state would be desirable], is not directly relevant to my argument and cannot be addressed here [...], on my view the answer is clearly yes." At the same time, most realists still find much sense in Kenneth Waltz's classic Cold War evaluation of world government in *Man, The State and War* (1959: 228): "And were world government attempted, we might find ourselves dying in the attempt, or uniting and living a life worse than death." But Kenneth Waltz never advised against U.S. participation in the United Nations, even though that institution might be seen as a "proto" world government that might ultimately become very powerful. Participation in international organizations obviously is not proscribed by the realist worldview; whether participation is or is not appropriate depends on the nature of the international organization.

Therefore, realist theory does not necessarily militate against participation in any and all world states—it depends on the proposed institutional characteristics and policy directions of the world state. Clearly, most U.S. realists would reject the proposal that the United States subject itself to the traditional world federalist ideal of the omnipotent world state: that it disarm itself entirely in order that the world state exercise monopoly control over all substantial armed forces and weapons of mass destruction. (But equally clearly, many if not most constructivists would also have reservations about this possibility, at least at the present moment in history.) At the same time, realist principles do not rule out participation in a "properly designed" world state, if by proper design is meant the incorporation of meaningful limitations on the power and authority of the world state, limitations sufficient to reduce the probability of a totalitarian outcome to an acceptable level, when weighed against the countervailing benefits. The important question is whether such a proper design exists, and if so, whether it will be recognized.

The Inevitability Proposition

To support the proposition that a world state is inevitable, Alexander Wendt deploys teleological reasoning. The author introduces this style of reasoning as follows (Wendt, 2003: 496):

> Teleological explanations explain by reference to an end or purpose toward which a system is directed. Like other explanations they are an-

> swers to a question [...], in this case "what is X for?" As such, they often take the grammatical form of "for the sake of" or "in order to" statements—Y is the final cause of X if X happens in order to realize Y. Ever since Francis Bacon, philosophers have tried to discredit such explanations as unscientific, and show that they can always be reduced to mechanical causation. Yet interest in teleology has recently come back. One reason is a widespread sense that efficient causation cannot account for apparent end-directedness in nature, so that some "explanatory structure" is lost if teleological reasoning is excluded altogether.

The resurgence of interest in teleology is especially prevalent in the field of biology. This is perhaps fitting, since biology studies living things, and all living things have purposes (basically to survive and thrive), even though they may not be consciously aware of these purposes. Furthermore, all individual living things follow a predictable, virtually inevitable, cycle of development through birth, growth, maturity, decline, and death. The biological cycle of development has been applied to human institutions as well, from corporations to empires.

Teleological reasoning comes naturally. All human beings have purposes, and all human artifacts have purposes. Thus we are very accustomed to the idea of purpose. Take clocks, for instance. A method for measuring time and dispersing information about the current time among the human population is extremely useful, even essential and vital, for the coordination of all sorts of human activity. Thus clocks were invented, and remain in continuous production, for this purpose. Similarly, the purpose of human clock-makers is to make clocks. That is, this is their purpose from the larger society's point of view. Individually, from their own point of view, the purpose of human clock-makers is the same as everyone else's: to survive and thrive.

But this idea of purpose is obviously human-centric, and confronts serious difficulties when applied to realities that are not the result of human intention. Consider the planet Earth, for example. An ancient philosopher, unaware of the size of the physical universe and accustomed to the notion of causation through divine intention, would be likely to proclaim that the purpose of planet Earth is to provide human beings with a place to live, i.e., that God created Earth for the benefit of humanity. Aside from the minority of highly enthusiastic adherents to one of the monotheistic religions of the world, this definition of the "purpose" of planet Earth would seem dubious to most contemporary minds. More common is the view that as a result of complex natural processes of which our understanding is quite limited, the universe came about, the planet Earth came about, humanity evolved and now lives on this planet.

Earth is useful to humanity, in fact it is vital to our survival. The Earth serves our (humanity's) purposes, but it did not come into being, in any larger, supra-human sense, for these purposes.

It seems a reasonable proposition that teleological thinking adds something to our understanding of reality. But whether it provides a meaningful alternative to so-called "mechanical" theories of causation is another question. While "mechanical" theories of causation are sometimes belittled as simplistic, superficial and naïve, such characterizations may be unfair. "Mechanical" causation might be anything but simple: there might be a thousand variables that enter into the determination of a single outcome, and only a few of them might be known and apparent to us. Thus an observed outcome may appear totally mysterious, unpredictable, even random—but that does not make it any less the result of a "mechanical" process linking cause(s) to effect. At most, therefore, teleological analysis might add something extra to our understanding of objects and events. But if it seems to be coming into direct conflict in any way with the principle of causation, then it is probably being misapplied.

By the principle of causation ("mechanical" causation, if one prefers), the current existence of the Earth was inevitable. It serves a human purpose, as a place of residence for our species. As suggested above, however, the fact that the Earth is useful to humanity did not guarantee its coming into being. Had the initial "big bang" that commenced the universe been slightly different, then the Earth would not have come about, at least in its present form. If, for example, the Earth had been similar to any of the other planets in our solar system (Mars, Venus, etc.), then humanity could not have evolved. It may well be that a properly designed world government would be extremely beneficial in terms of enhancing the future prospects of global human civilization (albeit this is a minority view at present). But the potential usefulness of world government for human purposes does not guarantee that it will come into being, any more than the usefulness of the planet Earth to human purposes guaranteed that it would come into being.

Although any given future outcome, whether it be the establishment of a world government or the outbreak of a nuclear World War III, is indeed inevitable in the strict sense according to the principle of causation, we cannot know for sure, at the present time, which particular future outcome will actually transpire. Presumably, however, on the assumption that most human beings are rationally pursuing what they perceive to be their best interests, the probability of any given future outcome is positively related to its desirability. The converse also holds: for example, we assume that a nuclear World War III is very unlikely because it would be so undesirable. By the same token, the more desirable a world government is perceived to be by humanity, the greater the likelihood that it will eventually be established. If world government comes to be perceived as *very* desirable by a great many people, then the probability of its creation would become very high—so high that we might contemplate use of the word "inevitable" to describe its prospects.

At the present time, of course, there is a very strong consensus among IR professionals, as well as among all other specific groups and the general population (excluding only the tiny minority of world federalist enthusiasts), that world government would be very *un*desirable. It is generally believed that world government would likely result in totalitarian tyranny, bureaucratic suffocation, cultural homogenization, or a combination of all three, along with possible additional dysfunctional outcomes. Moreover, efforts by individual nations to withdraw from the dysfunctional union would quite likely result in catastrophic civil warfare, quite possibly as destructive as the nuclear war the union was established to prevent. Wendt's essay represents an attempt to prod IR professionals into re-examining these widely and strongly held negative opinions about world government. This will be an uphill struggle. As Thomas Weiss (2009: 261) puts it:

> When someone like Campbell Craig (2008) notes the "resurgent idea of world government," this has more to do with the buzz about "global governance" and less with the serious mainstream discussion of supranationality per se. In fact, the subject of world government has been banned in sober and sensible discussion of global affairs and certainly is absent from classrooms. I cannot recall a single undergraduate or graduate student inquiring about the theoretical possibility of a central political authority exercising elements of universal legal jurisdiction. The surest way to secure classification as a crackpot is to mention a world government as either a hypothetical or, worse yet, desirable outcome.

Although the title of Professor Wendt's article undoubtedly possesses a certain shock value that may inspire many IR professionals to read it (if only to be able to refute it), certain aspects of the work could impede its effectiveness as a means of altering or modifying pre-conceived negative opinions about world government. To begin with, basing any proposition at all, let alone a proposition pertaining to world government, on teleological inevitability, is problematic. This is simply because it is doubtful whether teleology, as a mode of intellectual inquiry, has anything of substantial value to offer.

Moreover, while certain propositions involving the word "inevitable" are fairly acceptable (for example, that the Earth will continue to revolve around the Sun—barring a catastrophic collision with a large asteroid), assertions of inevitability applied to future outcomes that will be strongly influenced by (what appear to be) discretionary human actions, are far less acceptable. In fact, they rub many people the wrong way. Such assertions seem to imply that the asserter egotistically believes himself endowed with perfect predictive power. Outside the realm of religious faith, such a supernatural power is never attributed to mortal human beings. As a rule, the predictions of mortal human beings are not taken too seriously, for the simple reason that they are constantly being falsified by events.

Perhaps the most notorious case in modern history of faulty prediction was Karl Marx's prediction of the "inevitable" downfall of capitalism amid economic collapse and proletarian revolution. Although Marxist ideology was a major contributor to the Cold War confrontation that threatened global nuclear disaster during much of the second half of the twentieth century, it would be unfair to blame Karl Marx solely for the Cold War. The reigning national sovereignty system also played a role. Moreover, Marx's threats of proletarian revolution may have helped capitalist nations to soften and humanize their socioeconomic systems. But the fact remains that in light of the compelling empirical falsification of Marx's well-known prediction, as well as many other similar cases, assertions of the inevitability of any specific outcome in the future history of humanity are normally greeted with deep skepticism, if not outright derision.

Wendt offers skeptical readers of his inevitability essay two pieces of reasonably solid evidence that a world state will eventually be established: (1) the very long-run historical trend toward greater and greater political consolidation which has brought humanity from the tens of thousands of small, autonomous tribal units of pre-history down to the 200-odd nation-states of today, several of which encompass populations in the tens and even hundreds of millions; (2) the fact that a world state would benefit both large nations (lower probability of debilitating wars with other large nations) and small nations (lower probability of being subjected to the oppressive hegemony of large nations). Both of these points are significant and worthy of consideration, but in and of themselves, they are far from conclusive.

With respect to the long-term trend toward ever greater political consolidation, the hard fact remains that almost all of this consolidation was brought about, in one way or another, by means of warfare. In the nuclear age, it seems unlikely that additional warfare offers a plausible avenue toward further political consolidation leading to a world state. One must also take note of the fact that there has been a considerable amount of political de-consolidation in the recent past, ranging from the dissolution of the great European colonial empires to the disintegration of the Soviet Union and Yugoslavia. It is sometimes suggested that perhaps the most plausible scenario toward the creation of a world government is a nuclear world war that would so devastate global human civilization as to finally impress upon humanity the need for a strong world government. However, what may be more likely in the aftermath of a nuclear world war, would be a long period of low-intensity warfare fuelled by persistent bitterness and hostility, among a host of small states presided over by what are today referred to as "local warlords." A retrogressive trend might set in toward the same tens of thousands of small tribal units into which humanity was sub-divided prior to recorded history. The stage might be set for physical extinction of the species.

In presenting the consolidation evidence, Wendt (2003: 503) mentions the estimate of Robert Carneiro (1978) that in 1000 B.C. there were 600,000 independent political communities on the Earth, whereas today there are only about 200. It is interesting to note that in a more recent contribution ("The Political Unification of the World: Whether, When, and How—Some Speculations"), Carneiro summarizes his views as follows (2004: 162):

> That the world will someday be ruled by a single government has been foreseen by visionary thinkers for well more than a century, and this article quotes a number of these predictions. However, there has been less agreement as to how a world state would be achieved. Some have held that it would occur through peaceful and voluntary means. Others have argued that it could only result—as have all other political coalescences in the past—through military means. This article sides with the latter view and cites the war in Iraq as perhaps a small step in that direction.

As of 2004, when the above article was published, the war in Iraq had not yet fully degenerated into the quagmire it later became. In view of the adverse long-term aftermath of the 2003 invasion of Iraq, the notion of an "equivalent world government" through a relatively benign imperial hegemony imposed by the United States and its closest allies (Mandelbaum, 2005; Held and Koenig-Archibugi, 2004), has become even more doubtful than it was to begin with.

With respect to the potential benefits of world government for both the large nations and the small nations, it must be acknowledged that these are definite potential benefits, and need to be taken into account in any sensible evaluation of the world government possibility. But potential benefits have to be weighed against potential costs. The contemporary consensus is that the potential costs of world government (totalitarian tyranny, bureaucratic suffocation, global civil war) far exceed the potential benefits. Simply enumerating benefits, while paying little or no attention to costs, is unlikely to be rhetorically effective, given that the costs are so well known.

Two years following the appearance of Professor Wendt's 2003 inevitability essay, the *EJIR* published a critique (Shannon, 2005), to which the author replied (Wendt, 2005). The critique picked up on a potential flaw in the teleological argument that Wendt had himself anticipated in the concluding paragraphs of the 2003 paper: its potential neglect of the role of agency (human action) in the determination of outcomes. Shannon's complaint is that by casting the debate in terms of the *inevitability* of world government, Wendt is detracting from the more meaningful debate, involving agency and conditionality, concerning the *possibility* (i.e., desirability) of world government. Wendt's reply is that, when terms and concepts are properly understood, it is seen that there is no conflict between agency and teleology.

At possible cost to the subtleties of this exchange, it might be roughly compared to debate over the "free will" objection to "mechanical causation." Since we are unaware of all the multitude of factors pushing us to adopt a particular course of action, we have the impression that we have "free will" and could have, if we wanted, adopted a different course of action. The criminal justice system, for example, is based upon the perception that criminals are not forced, through Calvinist predestination, to commit crimes. The free will question is diverting, and debate over it is good intellectual and rhetorical exercise. But in the end, we are not likely to get beyond the following compromise: While the principle of causation does indeed rule out free will as it is normally understood, we do not know in advance what the principle of causation will bring about in any particular case of human decision-making; therefore, we perceive that we possess free will, and much of the existing social order is predicated upon this perception.

A similar formula would apply to agency and world government: While the principle of causation informs us either that it is inevitable that a world state *will* be part of future human history, or that it is inevitable that a world state *will not* be part of future human history, we do not know which of these outcomes will actually take place. Therefore, we operate on the basis that we (humanity in general) can make a free will choice between these two alternatives.

Between the U. N. and the Omnipotent World State

Prior to the successes of the Wright brothers and others in the early years of the twentieth century, it was a fairly commonplace speculation that the problems of heavier-than-air flight were too great ever to be overcome by human ingenuity. No less a scientific authority than William Thomson Kelvin (1824-1907), better known as Lord Kelvin, is reputed to have proclaimed in 1895: "Heavier-than-air flying machines are impossible" (Kaku, 2008). There are several problems involved in flight: lift, control, propulsion, power. Prior to the pioneers of the early twentieth century, several unsuccessful designs had been offered. A critical pre-condition for the successful solution of the overall problem was the development of small gasoline engines with a high ratio of power to weight. This solution to the power problem, in conjunction with solutions to the problems of lift, control and propulsion (wings, ailerons and rudders, propellers), made flight as we know it today possible. Whether or not heavier-than-air flying machines were possible could not have been determined on the basis of speculations employing the general scientific principles of the early twentieth century. It required a workable design involving solutions to the various problems of lift, control and propulsion, in combination with specific technological advances relevant to the power problem, to prove conclusively that heavier-than-air flying machines were indeed possible.

Something similar may be true with respect to world government. Whether or not a world government is possible (and desirable) may not be determinable on the basis of speculations based on general principles from political and other social sciences. The fact that these principles suggest that some world government schemes are unworkable does not necessarily establish that all world government schemes are unworkable. As gasoline engines turned out to be the solution to the power problem of flight at the turn of the twentieth century, possibly the technological advances that have produced contemporary communications and transportation will turn out to be the solution to the analogous "power problem" of world government at the turn of the twenty-first century. Even the most convinced world government skeptics have to concede that modern communications and transportation have rendered null and void the coordination problems of large-scale political organizations in the distant past. But instantaneous communications and rapid transportation do not, in themselves, make world government desirable or even possible. There are other problems that may or may not be solvable by means of a specific institutional design.

In current discussions of world government in the IR literature, there is very little attention paid to specific institutional characteristics of world government. Perhaps this has something to do with the injunction against "premature specificity" of Richard Falk (1975). Or perhaps it is because the editors and referees responsible for the professional literature have a low tolerance for institutional specifics pertaining to hypothetical world governments, feeling these to be more appropriate to science fiction than to scholarly discourse. This could be a dysfunctional attitude, in that specific design elements could be critical to whether world government could, or should, have a future in human history.

To the extent that mainstream IR authorities take any note of the world government possibility at all, it is normally abbreviated and dismissive. The following typical example is taken from *The New World Order* by Anne-Marie Slaughter (2004: 8):

> People and their governments around the world need global institutions to solve collective problems that can only be addressed on a global scale. They must be able to make and enforce global rules on a variety of subjects and through a variety of means... Yet world government is both infeasible and undesirable. The size and scope of such a government presents an unavoidable and dangerous threat to individual liberty. Further, the diversity of peoples to be governed makes it almost impossible to conceive of a global demos. No form of democracy within the current global repertoire seems capable of overcoming these obstacles.

This statement seems reasonable if it is presumed that the only form "world government" can take on is the world federalist ideal, termed here the "omnipotent world state." Although an embryonic notion of world government dates back to the ancient world (as empires endeavored unsuccessfully to extend their respective dominions over the "entire known world"), the modern notion of a full-purpose global government devoted not merely to peace-keeping but to human welfare-improving, only came to full fruition during the twentieth century, and more specifically during the ephemeral "world government boom" from 1945 through 1950. The devastation wrought by atomic bombs on the Japanese cities of Hiroshima and Nagasaki lent far more credence than ever before to the world federalist position that in the modern age, war has become too costly to continue to be an acceptable component of international relations. Humanity toyed, far more seriously than ever before, with the idea of establishing a universalist government embracing all of the peoples and nations of the world. Well-known intellectuals and statesmen declared their sympathetic interest in world government, and the level of grass-roots political activism in pursuit of this goal reached unprecedented levels (Heater, 1996; Harris, 1999; Baratta, 2004). The boom was soon deflated, the victim of the quickly developing, ideologically charged strategic confrontation between the communist nations and the noncommunist nations. By the outbreak of the Korean War in 1950, all but the most diehard world federalists were resigned to the reality that the window of opportunity had been closed (Mangone, 1951; Schuman, 1952).

Although post-World War II world government proposals are highly diverse, most of them adhere in general terms to the Declaration of the first World Congress of the World Movement for World Federal Government, held in 1947 at Montreux, Switzerland. The Declaration puts forward six essential characteristics of an effective world government, as follows:

1. Universal membership: The world federal government must be open to all peoples and nations.
2. Limitations of national sovereignty, and the transfer to the world federal government of such legislative, executive and judicial powers as relate to world affairs.
3. Enforcement of world law directly on the individual whoever or wherever he may be, within the jurisdiction of the world federal government: guarantee of the rights of man and suppression of all attempts against the security of the federation.
4. Creation of supranational armed forces capable of guaranteeing the security of the world federal government and of its member states. Disarmament of member nations to the level of their internal policing requirements.
5. Ownership and control by the world federal government of atomic development and of other scientific discoveries capable of mass destruction.
6. Power to raise adequate revenues directly and independently of state taxes.

Point 1 specifies that there be "universal membership" in the sense that membership would be "open" to all the nations of the world. Nothing is specified, however, with respect to nations that join the world federation and then decide at a later date to withdraw. However, a phrase included in point 3 ("suppression of all attempts against the security of the federation") may well be directed against such nations. This would be consistent with the well-remembered fact (in 1947) that one of the first indications of the aggressive intentions of Nazi Germany and the other fascist nations was their withdrawal from the League of Nations. At any rate, a "right of withdrawal" would be essentially meaningless if nations had no armed forces with which to back up their decision to withdraw from the world federation. And in points 4 and 5, it is clearly specified that the member nations of the world federation would be deprived of all heavy weaponry (i.e., weaponry beyond the requirements of "internal policing"), both nuclear and conventional.

Of the various world government institutional blueprints inspired by the postwar boom, only a few achieved anything beyond vestigial recognition. Among these may be included the proposal of the University of Chicago "Provisional Committee to Frame a World Constitution" for a Federal Republic of the World (Hutchins, 1948, 1949; Borgese, 1953), the proposal of Clark and Sohn for a strengthened United Nations (Clark and Sohn, 1966), and the proposal of the World Constitution and Parliament Association for a Federation of Earth (Isely, 1993, 1999). These proposals are typical of the traditional world federalist ideal of the omnipotent world state in three critical respects.

First, the world legislature follows commendably democratic principles, with the inevitable result that representatives from the relatively poor nations of the world would dominate the voting. These representatives might have a strong predisposition toward radical global income redistribution. Second, membership in the world federation would be universal, permanent and irreversible. Any movement by a member nation toward withdrawing from the world federation would be viewed as treasonous and met by force. Therefore, rich nations unwilling to participate in a radical global income redistribution project undertaken by the world federation would not be able to legally and peacefully leave the federation. Third, member nations would be fully disarmed, and all large-scale military forces and heavy armament would be concentrated under the authority of the world federation. As Clark and Sohn (1966: xv) put it:

> The complete disarmament of all the nations (rather than the mere "reduction" or "limitation" of armaments) is essential for any solid and lasting peace, this disarmament to be accomplished in a simultaneous and proportionate manner by carefully verified stages and subject to a well-organized system of inspection. It is now generally accepted that disarmament must be universal and enforceable. That it must also be complete is no less necessary, since: (a) in the nuclear age no mere reduction in the new means of mass destruction could be effective to remove fear and tension; and (b) if any substantial national armaments were to remain, even if only ten per cent of the armaments of 1960, it would be impracticable to maintain a sufficiently strong world police force to deal with any possible aggression or revolt against the authority of the world organization. We should face the fact that until there is *complete* disarmament of every nation without exception there can be no assurance of genuine peace.

What this means is that if the world federation were to undertake a radical global income redistribution project, rich nations unwilling to participate in this project and desirous of leaving the federation, would possess no military power with which to support this desire.

A potential attempt by the world government to establish and enforce a highly redistributive global welfare state is merely an example of what might go wrong. A natural concern of citizens of the poorer nations of the world is that, whatever might be the distribution of formal voting weights, in practice the wealthy nations would somehow exert their influence to establish and enforce an international trade and investment regime that would essentially duplicate the exploitative economic relationships between rich and poor nations of the colonial era. And aside from economics, there are numerous political, religious and cultural differences among the nations that might cause problems.

Is assumed by most IR professionals, with little or no reflection, that these problems are beyond solution, and therefore a world government is, in Anne-Marie Slaughter's words, "both infeasible and undesirable." This assumption is questionable, if one considers institutional alternatives lying somewhere between the relatively ineffectual United Nations of today, and the omnipotent world state envisioned in conventional world federalist thinking. These alternatives are sometimes hinted at in the IR literature. For example, in his inevitability essay, Alexander Wendt offers the following thoughts (2003: 506):

> Lest I be accused of lacking imagination, however, it should be emphasized that the systemic changes needed for a world state could be fulfilled in various ways, and so a world state might look very different than states today. In particular, it could be much more decentralized, in three respects. First, it would not require its elements to give up local autonomy. Collectivizing organized violence does not mean that culture, economy or local politics must be collectivized; subsidiarity could be the operative principle. Second, it would not require a single UN army. As long as a structure exists that can command and enforce a collective response to threats, a world state could be compatible with the existence of national armies, to which enforcement operations might be sub-contracted (along the lines of NATO perhaps). Finally, it would not even require a world "government", if by this we mean a unitary body with one leader whose decisions are final (cf. Bull's [1977] "domestic analogy"). As long as binding choices can be made, decision-making in a world state could involve broad deliberation in a "strong" public sphere rather than command by one person.

With respect to the third point, virtually all world government proposals are adamant that any form of dictatorship or oligarchy must be strictly avoided, and are insistent that each and every citizen of the federation possess significant voting weight in electing high state officials. With respect to the first point, virtually all world government proposals envision a federal structure in which the component nations would retain substantial autonomy (i.e., sovereignty) with respect to all domestic public choice matters that do not impinge heavily on the interests of other nations. It is the second point that is the most weighty: the suggestion that a world state need not require the full disarmament of component nations. This is definitely *not* in line with the omnipotent world state concept, as set forth by Clark and Sohn and many like-minded others.

Given the nationalistic attitudes that persist throughout the world, especially in the major military powers, it is most likely a necessary condition to make an actual world federation even minimally feasible in the real world that its component nations be allowed to retain their own independent and autonomous armed forces. At this point I will put forward an innovative proposal for a full-fledged world government approximately halfway between the existent United Nations of today and the omnipotent world state of traditional world federalist thinking. For convenience, this hypothetical state entity will be provisionally designated the World Federal Union (WFU).

The WFU would be a legitimate state entity, its government composed of legislative, executive, and judicial branches, the officials of all three branches being subject to democratic election. Although democratic accountability is a fundamental long-term objective, no nation would be denied membership on the basis of failing to implement the democratic procedures common to the United States, Japan, the Western European nations, and other fully democratic nations around the world. The only membership requirement for nations such as the People's Republic of China and many others, would be their agreement to eventually implement fully democratic practices once their citizens have been properly prepared for their responsibilities under this system. No time frame would be specified for such "proper preparation."

It is proposed that the World Federal Union display the standard trappings and emblems of state power (capital city, flag, anthem, etc.), that it possess a significant degree of coercive power (including some military forces under its permanent, direct command), that it exercise meaningful legislative authority through the passage and enforcement of global laws (including those pertaining to taxation), and that it become a major player in the institutions and processes of global governance (for example, by incorporating various specialized agencies of the United Nations). Applying the well-worn humorism ("If it looks like a duck and walks like a duck, then it probably *is* a duck"), it can be said that since the WFU "looks like a state and acts like a state, then it probably *is* a state."

There are two critical aspects of the proposal, however, that are definitely *not* consistent with the contemporary concept of the national state: (1) member nations would retain the permanent and irrevocable right to withdraw from the Federal Union at their unilateral discretion; (2) member nations would retain the permanent and irrevocable right to maintain as large a military force as they desire under their independent and autonomous control, armed with as much heavy weaponry as is deemed necessary (including nuclear weapons). The "open door" policy means that once the Union is formed, it might soon thereafter disintegrate as nations find intolerable the inevitable constraints placed on their sovereignty through participation in the federation. But without this policy, the world government will almost certainly not be established in the first place; if, however, the world government is established with this policy in place, there is a reasonable probability that the federation will be successful and the "right to withdrawal" will eventually become a dead letter. However, it has to be recognized that with such a policy, it is almost certain that some nations, including possibly some large and powerful nations, will remain outside the federation for a period of time, possibly a lengthy period of time. Although this will clearly reduce the effectiveness of the world federation in the short term, it will not eliminate it.

Equally as fundamental as the "open door" policy is the allowance for independent armed forces of the component nations. This, of course, is diametrically and dramatically opposed to the omnipotent world state concept. There would be no expectation that nations would disarm, even to a minimal extent, upon joining the federation. Most likely, many nations, especially the large and militarily powerful nations, would retain their existing armed forces for many years or even decades following the formation of the union. The hope is that the federation will be successful, that the member nations will become gradually more confident of the trustworthiness and good will of the other member nations, and that consequently disarmament will gradually occur, at whatever pace with which the nations are comfortable. The argument, once again, is that without this provision, which is a necessary guarantor of the open door policy, the world government will never be established in the first place, and will never have an opportunity to prove itself.

Since the decline of ideological conflict with the ending of the Cold War, the North-South economic gap has taken over as the single most important impediment to stable and benign world government in the long term. The WFU proposal involves both a short-term political expedient to cope with the problem, and a long-term economic program to eliminate the problem. The short-term political expedient is a "dual voting" system: whenever a vote is taken in the federation legislature, the measure being considered would have to be approved by a majority, possibly greater than a 50 percent majority, on two different bases: the population basis and the material basis. In the population vote, the weight given to the vote of each particular representative would be proportional to the population of his/her district, relative to the total population of the Federal Union. In the material vote, the weight given to the vote of each particular representative would be proportional to the financial revenues derived from his/her district, relative to the total financial revenues of the Federal Union. This system would prevent the passage of legislation aimed at a drastic redistribution of current world income (which would be opposed by the rich nations), and it would also prevent the passage of legislation that might be viewed as re-establishing conditions of colonial exploitation (which would be opposed by the poor nations).

The possibility obviously exists that the dual voting system would give rise to "legislative gridlock," preventing the passage of all but the most trivial global legislation. However, it is questionable whether gridlock would be worse, in practical terms, than it is currently without a world government in operation. The practical relevance of the distinction between the population vote and the material vote would be eliminated were all nations of the world to have approximately equal per capita income. This condition would be the long-term objective of the complementary economic proposal for a long-term economic program, in effect a Global Marshall Plan (GMP), to eliminate, or at least greatly reduce, the very large gap between economic living standards in the richest nations, and those in the poorest. This basic idea has a lengthy pedigree in visionary thinking (Barr, 1950, 1953; Church, 1978), and is currently being pushed by the Global Marshall Plan Initiative, a pressure group active in Western Europe (Petit, 2008; Mayton, 2009).

Under a full-fledged GMP, nations such as the United States, Japan, the Western European nations, and other wealthy nations, would contribute in the range from two to four percent of their Gross National Products to a transfer fund for the purpose of increasing the generalized capital stocks of the recipient nations (business physical capital, human capital, and social overhead capital). These contributions would be much greater than existing contributions, but may be within the range of political feasibility, since military expenditures currently account for substantially larger percentages of GNP, especially for the superpowers. Such a program might result in a dramatic narrowing of the economic gap at the relatively minor cost to the donor nations of a modest decrease in the rate of rise of their per capita incomes.

Whether or not a Global Marshall Plan would succeed in its purposes cannot be predicted with any confidence at the present time, simply because nothing like it has ever been tried. I would suggest that the GMP be undertaken on a tentative and provisional basis, with the understanding that if after a reasonable trial period between 10 and 20 years, the program is not making significant progress in narrowing the global economic gap, then it will be gradually downsized and eventually terminated. Since it cannot be reliably determined whether or not a Global Marshall Plan would be successful, the only way to answer this question in a scientific manner is to apply the experimental method: to initiate the program and observe the outcome.

Clearly, this trial-and-error approach also applies to the World Federal Union itself. If it is established, and afterward fails to make a positive contribution to global governance, then the open door policy allows for its peaceful dissolution. Humanity would be back to where we are today, sadder but wiser, and otherwise none the worse for wear. Some lessons will have been learned that might be valuable in the future. In the past, much of human progress has been through trial and error, and this situation will no doubt continue in the future. If we envision world government in these terms, clearly the risks of proceeding into the future with a world government are very significantly less than they would be if the world government was to be necessarily a permanent and omnipotent polity.

Conclusion

The term "global governance" rose to prominence in the years immediately following the renunciation of Marxist ideology by the USSR and its Eastern European satellites in the early 1990s. Ostensibly, all the successor nations to the USSR, and all the ex-communist Eastern European nations, now have no quarrel whatsoever with capitalism, the market system, and political democracy, and in fact very much desire to cultivate these institutions themselves. No longer is the capitalist economic system and the democratic political system under ideological assault by a nuclear superpower. Relations between the United States and the Russian Federation, while still somewhat stiff and restrained, are amicable enough on the surface, especially in view of what went on before. The second communist superpower of the Cold War period, the People's Republic of China, did not renounce communism, and at the present time it is neither democratic nor capitalist in the strict sense. However, its dynamic market socialist economic system is unrecognizably distant from the central planning of traditional communism. Moreover, whatever long-term national goals may be envisioned by the present-day communist leadership of the PRC, for the moment at least these goals apparently do not include exporting the Chinese socioeconomic system to the rest of the world.

The waning of the ideological confrontation among the superpower nations enabled a higher level of international cooperation in dealing with global problems than had been achieved during the Cold War, during which progressive initiatives from one side of the ideological confrontation were frequently blocked by the other side on the basis of generalized suspicion and hostility. In the early 1990s, therefore, the idea arose and developed that absent the ideological problem, international cooperation through the United Nations and other international organizations could advance to such a high level that the results would be comparable to what would be achieved if there were an actual world government in operation. This idea has been explored in numerous contributions in the IR literature, exemplified by Paolini et al (1998), Hewson and Sinclair (1999), Sinclair (2004), and Wilkinson and Hughes (2004). If indeed it is true that effective global governance can be achieved without effective global government, then this is fortunate since, in the consensus view, an actual world government is still impractical despite the easing of the ideological problem.

According to the realist dictum of Kenneth Waltz (1959: 228): "The amount of force needed to hold a society together varies with the heterogeneity of the elements composing it." During the Cold War decades, the most obvious element of heterogeneity was the ideological gap between the communist and noncommunist nations. In the opinion of Waltz and virtually all other international relations authorities during these decades, ideological heterogeneity, in and of itself, precluded world government. Thus far in the post-Cold War era, it is believed by the large majority of IR authorities that world government is still precluded, owing to remaining ideological issues (such as the absence of democratic institutions in the PRC), together with an array of economic, religious, cultural, linguistic and racial heterogeneities.

Of these, arguably North-South economic heterogeneity is most important. The Cold War decades created in humanity far greater consciousness than ever before of the global economic gap, the tremendous gulf that separates the high living standards in the minority of rich nations from the low living standards in the majority of poor nations. This economic gap was a major factor in the geopolitical situation during the Cold War, as both the wealthier capitalist nations and the communist nations endeavored to win over the nonaligned Third World nations to their respective sides of the ideological conflict. According to World

Bank statistical data, most of the Third World nations made respectable gains in per capita income during the latter part of the twentieth century, the major exception being the nations of sub-Saharan Africa. On the other hand, economic growth has, on the whole, been stronger in the richest nations, with the consequence that the gap between the richest nations and the poorest nations has been getting wider.

During the Cold War, the noncommunist nations were leery of world government on grounds (among other things) that it might be subverted by the communist nations and transformed into a tool of communist expansionism. At the same time, the communist nations were leery of world government on grounds (among other things) that it might be subverted (from their point of view) and transformed into a tool of capitalistic reaction. Now that the Cold War has faded, the rich nations are leery of world government on grounds that it might be controlled by the poor nations and transformed into a tool for the radical transfer of current income from the rich nations to the poor nations. Meanwhile, the poor nations are leery of world government on grounds that it might be controlled by the rich nations and transformed into a tool for the reestablishment of colonial-style economic exploitation of the poor nations. Such apprehensions are understandable if it is assumed that a world government must necessarily conform to the world federalist ideal of the omnipotent world state. As emphasized here, however, there are alternative world government possibilities, less centralized and powerful than the omnipotent world state, under which neither a global welfare state nor a return to colonial exploitation would be likely.

In his international relations textbook, Mark Amstutz concludes his treatment of world federalism as follows (1999: 329):

> A stable world government needs a centralized governmental structure and widespread shared values and aspirations. A world federal regime will require the creation of both a central authority and strong social, economic, cultural, and political affinities. The dilemma of world government is this: the international system needs world government to reduce the threat of war, but the precondition for world government is world community, which can only be solidified through the political transformation of the anarchic world system.

The argument here is that world community, as defined by "widespread shared values and aspirations" and "strong social, economic, cultural, and political affinities," is a pre-condition for world government, and since world community does not yet exist, world government is therefore impractical. The problem with this argument is that it fails to appreciate gradations in both world community and world government, and also the possibility of dynamic interaction between the two. While the currently existing level of world community is insufficient to support an *unlimited* world government (the omnipotent world state), it may be sufficient to support a *limited* world government. Once a limited world government has been established, it might then evolve, by gradual stages, toward a more authoritative and effective government authority.

Consider the traditional question: Which came first: the chicken or the egg? What makes the question absurd, and therefore humorous, is that neither the modern chicken nor the modern egg came first. The modern chicken-egg-chicken progression is the result of millions of years of evolutionary development with roots in the primeval slime. Those who would argue that it is necessary to have a high level of homogeneity prior to having an effective state are equivalent to those who would argue, in response to the chicken-egg question, that since chickens come out of eggs, then the egg came first. The problem with this argument, obviously, is that it is also true that eggs come out of chickens. If we take social and attitudinal homogeneity to be the egg, and the effectiveness of state organization to be the chicken, the relevance of the chicken-egg question becomes clear. A population which is politically united within the same state organization tends to become, over time, more socially and attitudinally homogeneous. Similarly, as a given population becomes more socially and attitudinally homogeneous, its state organization tends to become more effective. There is a progressive, interactive, mutually reinforcing, snowballing process between the social and attitudinal homogeneity of a given population, and the effectiveness of the state organization in which it is politically united.

It is quite obvious, to all but the most enthusiastic world federalists, that the degree of homogeneity among nations today is insufficient to support a world state with an amount of practical and moral authority over the nations of the world analogous to that of the national government of the United States today over the 50 states. This means that an *extremely* powerful, effective and authoritative world state is an impossibility at the present time. It does not mean that a *somewhat* powerful, effective and authoritative world state is an impossibility at the present time. Quite possibly a limited world government, of the sort discussed above, would in fact be acceptable to many if not most nations in the world today—if and when they become aware of this alternative. Once a limited world government has been established, it might then commence a long-term process of gradual evolution toward a higher level of homogeneity among its citizens, and a higher level of effectiveness in its operations.

If global governance is what we have had over the last 20 years since the ebbing of the Cold War in the early 1990s, clearly this system falls short of what we had hoped for. The superpowers still feel it necessary to maintain large armed forces equipped with nuclear weapons. Some small, non-nuclear nations ("rogue" nations) are endlessly fascinated by the prospect of acquiring such weapons, as are terrorist groups desirous of surpassing the 9/11 success of Al-Qaeda. See, for example: Utgoff (2000); Allison (2004), Levi (2007), Kessler (2007), Suskind (2008), Jenkins (2008), Caravelli (2008), Stevenson (2008). This raises concern over such questions, for example, as just how far the other nuclear powers will allow the United States and its allies to go in quest of security against nuclear proliferation and nuclear terrorism.

Leaving aside apocalyptic visions, localized conflict situations (as in Rwanda, Bosnia, Darfur and elsewhere) continue to produce much human misery, the population explosion throughout the world over the last century is putting ever-greater pressure on both the natural resource base and the purity of the natural environment, the AIDS crisis has reminded us of our potential vulnerability to catastrophic epidemics of contagious diseases. These are global problems in that they have important ramifications in almost every nation on the planet. The extent to which humanity will be able to cope effectively with these problems is critically affected by the predisposition among nations toward mutual respect, trust and cooperation. The persistence of us-versus-them attitudes in the various national populations makes it difficult for national governments to reach binding agreements on global problems.

Aside from a small minority of anarchists, the usefulness of formal government is fully acknowledged. Government is considered beneficial at the local level, the regional level, and the national level. This suggests the possibility that government could also be beneficial at the global level. The *potential* desirability of a properly designed world government is more or less self-evident. Global government would not *necessarily* enable us to cope effectively with global problems, but it might well do better in this regard than the existing international regime.

Yet in the hundreds of articles and dozens of books published every year in the popular and professional literature on contemporary international relations, terms such as "world government," "global government," "world state," and the like, rarely appear, and when they do, more often than not it is in the course of a cursory dismissal such as that of Anne-Marie Slaughter (2004: 8) quoted above. Nevertheless, Campbell Craig (2008) writes of a recent "resurgence" of interest in world government. What evidence is there for this alleged resurgence? To begin with, we might possibly be in the midst of a spike in the production of appeals for world government from world federalist enthusiasts whose strident "one world or none" message harks back to the 1945-50 world government boom. Examples include Tetalman and Belitsos (2005), Harris (2005), Martin (2008), and Stark (2008). Of course, if appeals of this nature went unheeded during the perilous decades of the Cold War, they are even less likely to be effective now that the Cold War is history and the threat of nuclear world war in the near future has greatly receded.

What may be more significant is that a trickle has begun of more restrained and scholarly world government advocacies from authors with reputable academic credentials, as exemplified by Cabrera (2004), Pojman (2006), and Tännsjö (2008). While these more reflective and balanced advocacies are more likely to elicit serious interest in world government among those who are currently skeptical of the concept, the fact remains that they are still very few in number. Moreover, they are generally rather vague on the institutional specifics of the world government being advocated. Advocacies that focus on the various potential benefits of world government while paying insufficient attention to the potential costs, specifically to the danger that an omnipotent world state, of the sort envisioned in conventional world federalist thought, might soon evolve into a totalitarian tyranny in the mode of Hitler's Germany and Stalin's Russia, are unlikely to be taken seriously by most mainstream IR professionals.

The situation might well be considerably different if the focus were shifted explicitly from the omnipotent world state concept toward a limited world state concept. The potential costs of the latter are significantly lower than the potential costs of the former, from which it follows that the ratio of potential benefits to potential costs of world government would be significantly improved under the latter. The potential significance of a properly designed supernational federation to the future prospects of humanity is obviously very great. There is no profession better trained to tackle the "proper design" question than the international relations profession.

References

Allison, Graham. *Nuclear Terrorism: The Ultimate Preventable Catastrophe.* New York: Henry Holt, 2004.

Amstutz, Mark R. *International Conflict and Cooperation: An Introduction to World Politics.* New York: McGraw-Hill College, 1999.

Baratta, Joseph P. *The Politics of World Federation.* Vol. I: *United Nations, UN Reform, Atomic Control.* Vol. II: *From World Federalism to Global Governance.* Westport, Conn.: Praeger, 2004.

Barr, Stringfellow. *Let's Join the Human Race.* Chicago: University of Chicago Press, 1950.

Barr, Stringfellow. *Citizens of the World.* Garden City, NY: Doubleday, 1953.

Borgese, Giuseppe A. *Foundations of the World Republic.* Chicago: University of Chicago Press, 1953.

Bull, Hedley. *The Anarchical Society: A Study of Order in World Politics.* New York: Columbia University Press, 1977.

Cabrera, Luis. *Political Theory of Global Justice: A Cosmopolitan Case for the World State.* New York: Routledge, 2004.

Caravelli, Jack. *Nuclear Insecurity: Understanding the Threat from Rogue Nations and Terrorists.* Westport, Conn.: Praeger, 2008.

Carneiro, Robert L. "Political Expansion as an Expression of the Principle of Competitive Exclusion," in Ronald Cohen and Elman Service, eds., *Origins of the State* (Philadelphia: Institute for the Study of Human Issues, 1978).

Carneiro, Robert L. "The Political Unification of the World: Whether, When, and How—Some Speculations," *Cross-Cultural Research* 38(2): 162-177, May 2004.

Church, George J. "The Case for a Global Marshall Plan," *Time*, June 12, 1978.

Clark, Grenville, and Louis B. Sohn, *World Peace through World Law*, third enlarged edition, Cambridge, Mass.: Harvard University Press, 1966.

Craig, Campbell. "The Resurgent Idea of World Government," *Ethics & International Affairs* 22(2): 133-142, Summer 2008.

Finnemore, Martha. *National Interests in International Society.* New York: Cornell University Press, 1996.

Hall, Rodney Bruce. *National Collective Identity: Social Constructs and International Systems.* New York: Columbia University Press, 1999.

Harris, Errol E., "Summary Outline History of World Federalism," in Errol E. Harris and James A. Yunker, eds., *Toward Genuine Global Governance: Critical Reactions to Our Global Neighborhood* (Westport, Conn.: Praeger Publishers, 1999).

Harris, Errol E. *Earth Federation Now: Tomorrow Is Too Late.* Radford, Va.: Institute for Economic Democracy, 2005.

Heater, Derek. *World Citizenship and Government: Cosmopolitan Ideas in the History of Western Political Thought.* New York: St. Martin's Press, 1996.

Held, David, and Mathias Koenig-Archibugi, eds. *American Power in the Twenty-First Century.* Malden, Mass.: Polity Press, 2004.

Herz, John H. *The Nation-State and the Crisis of World Politics: Essays on International Politics in the Twentieth Century.* New York: David McKay, 1976.

Hewson, Martin, and Timothy J. Sinclair, eds. *Approaches to Global Governance Theory.* Albany, NY: State University of New York Press, 1999.

Hutchins, Robert M., et al. *Preliminary Draft of a World Constitution.* Chicago: University of Chicago Press, 1948.

Hutchins, Robert M. *Foundations for World Order.* Denver: University of Denver Press, 1949.

Isely, Philip, et al. "A Constitution for the Federation of Earth," in Errol E. Harris, *One World or None: Prescription for Surviva l* (Atlantic Highlands, NJ: Humanities Press, 1993).

Isley, Philip. "A Critique of Our Global Neighborhood," in Errol E. Harris and James A. Yunker, editors, *Toward Genuine Global Governance: Critical Reactions to Our Global Neighborhood* (Westport, Conn.: Praeger Publishers, 1999).

Jenkins, Brian Michael. *Will Terrorists Go Nuclear?* Amherst, NY: Prometheus Books, 2008.

Kaku, Michio. *Physics of the Impossible: A Scientific Exploration into the World of Phasers, Force Fields, Teleportation, and Time Travel.* New York: Doubleday, 2008.

Katzenstein, Peter J., ed. *The Culture of National Security: Norms and Identity in World Politics.* New York: Columbia University Press, 1996.

Kessler, Ronald. *The Terrorist Watch: Inside the Desperate Race to Stop the Next Attack.* New York: Crown Forum, 2007.

Levi, Michael A. *On Nuclear Terrorism.* Cambridge, Mass.: Harvard University Press, 2007.

Mandelbaum, Michael. *The Case for Goliath: How America Acts as the World's Government in the 21st Century.* New York: Public Affairs Press, 2005.

Mangone, Gerald J. *The Idea and Practice of World Government.* New York: Columbia University Press, 1951.

Martin, Glen T. *Ascent to Freedom: Practical and Philosophical Foundations of Democratic World Law.* Sun City, Arizona: Institute for Economic Democracy Press, 2008.

Mayton, Daniel. *Nonviolence and Peace Psychology.* New York: Springer, 2009.

Niebuhr, Reinhold. *The Structure of Nations and Empires: A Study of the Recurring Patterns and Problems of the Political Order in Relation to the Unique Problems of the Nuclear Age.* New York: Scribner, 1959.

Paolini, Albert J., Anthony P. Jarvis, and Christian Reus-Smit, eds. *Between Sovereignty and Global Governance: The United Nations, the State and Civil Society.* New York: St. Martin's Press, 1998.

Petit, Patrick U. *Earthrise: The Dawning of a New Civilization in the 21st Century.* Munich: Herbert Utz Verlag, 2008.

Pojman, Louis P. *Terrorism, Human Rights, and the Case for World Government.* Lanham, Md.: Rowman & Littlefield, 2006.

Posner, Eric A. "International Law: A Welfarist Approach," *University of Chicago Law Review* 73(2): 487-543, Spring 2006.

Richard Falk, "A New Paradigm for International Legal Studies: Prospects and Proposals," *Yale Law Journal* 84(5): 969-1021, April 1975.

Schuman, Frederick L. *The Commonwealth of Man: An Inquiry into Power Politics and World Government.* New York: Alfred A. Knopf, 1952.

Shannon, Vaughn P. "Wendt's Violation of the Constructivist Project: Agency and Why a World State is *Not* Inevitable," *European Journal of International Relations* 11(4): 581-587, October 2005.

Sinclair, Timothy, ed. *Global Governance: Critical Concepts in Political Science.* New York: Routledge, 2004.

Slaughter, Anne-Marie. *A New World Order.* Princeton, NJ: Princeton University Press, 2004.

Stark, Jim. *Rescue Plan for Planet Earth: Democratic World Government through a Global Referendum.* Toronto: Key Publishing House, 2008.

Stevenson, Jonathan. *Thinking beyond the Unthinkable: Harnessing Doom from the Cold War to the War on Terror.* New York: Viking, 2008.

Suskind, Ron. *The Way of the World: A Story of Truth and Hope in an Age of Extremism.* New York: HarperCollins, 2008.

Tännsjö, Torbjörn. *Global Democracy: The Case for a World Government.* Edinburgh: Edinburgh University Press, 2008.

Tetalman, Jerry, and Byron Belitsos. *One World Democracy: A Progressive Vision for Enforceable World Law.* San Rafael, California: Origin Press, 2005.

Utgoff, Victor A., ed. *The Coming Crisis: Nuclear Proliferation, U.S. Interests, and World Order.* Cambridge, Mass.: MIT Press, 2000.

Waltz, Kenneth N. *Man, the State and War.* New York: Columbia University Press, 1959.

Waltz, Kenneth N. *Theory of International Politics.* New York: McGraw-Hill, 1979.

Waltz, Kenneth N. *Realism and International Politics: The Essays of Ken Waltz.* New York: Taylor & Francis, 2008.

Weiss, Thomas G. "What Happened to the Idea of World Government," *International Studies Quarterly* 53(2): 253-271, June 2009.

Wendt, Alexander. "Anarchy Is What States Make of It," *International Organization* 46(2): 399-403, Spring 1992.

Wendt, Alexander. *Social Theory of International Politics.* Cambridge, U.K.: Cambridge University Press, 1999.

Wendt, Alexander. "Why a World State Is Inevitable," *European Journal of International Relations* 9(4): 491-542, October 2003.

Wendt, Alexander. "Agency, Teleology, and the World State: A Reply to Shannon," *European Journal of International Relations* 11(4): 589-598, October 2005.

Wight, Martin. *Power Politics*, 2nd edition (Hedley Bull, Carsten Holbraad, eds.). New York: Viking Penguin, 1978.

Wilkinson, Rorden, and Stephen Hughes, eds. *Global Governance: Critical Perspectives.* New York: Routledge, 2002.

3

Evolutionary World Government

Introduction

The currently prevailing concept of world government, among both the large majority of world government skeptics and the small minority of world government supporters (the "world federalists"), is that of a very strong state entity that would stand in relation to its component member nations much as the federal government of the United States stands in relation to the fifty component states. Such a government would encompass all nations in the world without exception, would not tolerate the withdrawal of any nation from the federation under any circumstance, and would monopolize all heavy weaponry, including nuclear weapons. This concept of world government is referred to here as the "omnipotent world state." In addition, the world government would be subject to pure democratic control by its citizens through free and contested election of high government officials. According to proponents, such a government would virtually eliminate the possibility of nuclear holocaust, and would enable effective global action to be taken against such long-term threats as economic inequality and environmental deterioration. According to skeptics, such a government would either quickly dissolve amidst civil war, or it would stabilize itself by means of imposing a draconic totalitarian regime on the world, most likely of a dictatorial nature.

Aside from the small minority of world federalists, it is almost universally assumed that there is no credible transition path, of a peaceful nature, from the current international status quo to the omnipotent world state described above. This essay does not challenge this consensus opinion. However, it does challenge the widespread view that no federal world government short of the omnipotent world state would be a worthwhile undertaking. The basis of the challenge is the proposition that there exist viable world government possibilities whose authority and effectiveness would lie somewhere between that of today's relatively ineffectual United Nations, and that of the omnipotent world state, and that these intermediate possibilities would both significantly improve the processes of global governance in the proximate future, as well as laying a secure foundation for further gradual, evolutionary progress over the long term toward a highly authoritative and effective, yet democratic and benign, world government. In other words, a limited world government, as opposed to an unlimited world government, is both achievable and desirable. Or at least a more persuasive case can be made to this effect than can be made for the omnipotent world state. In fact, it is arguable that were the notion of limited world government to become sufficiently familiar to the international relations profession and the general public, this might result in such a fundamental reappraisal of the general concept of world government that the establishment of an actual world government within the foreseeable future would become significantly more likely.

In support of this proposition, this essay explores the analogy between "evolutionary socialism" and "evolutionary world government." At the turn of the twentieth century, such revisionist socialists as Eduard Bernstein laid a secure foundation for the increasing success of social democracy during the twentieth century in Western Europe and throughout the world, by means of redefining the objectives of socialism, and by rethinking the strategy for attaining these objectives. By revising the orthodox Marxist concept of socialism, and renouncing the orthodox Marxist doctrine of the necessity of violent revolution to achieve socialism, the revisionists made this new concept of socialism more attractive to a broad range of the population. It is possible that in the twenty-first century, an analogous revision of the world federalist objective away from the omnipotent world state and toward a limited federal world government, would lay the basis for a viable and effective real-world political movement toward this revised objective. On the basis of real-world experience, it is now widely accepted that many if not most of the institutions and policies associated with social democracy have had a generally beneficial effect on the welfare of most of the world's population. If in the future a limited world government were to be established in the real world and given time to prove itself, it might at some point thereafter be widely acknowledged as having significantly improved the welfare of most if not all of the world's population.

The remainder of this essay is organized as follows. First, a brief history of the idea of world government is presented, with special emphasis on the rise and fall of the world federalist movement in the aftermath of World War II. It is proposed that the rapid decline of world federalism into political insignificance during the postwar period is largely attributable to the inability of both proponents and opponents, in both the noncommunist and communist nations, to conceive of world government as anything other than the omnipotent world state. We proceed to a brief account of the socialist movement from its origins in the early nineteenth century to the present day. A pivotal point in this history was the recognition by a significant number of socialists, toward the end of the nineteenth century, that a viable alternative existed to the hard-line Marxist concept of socialism, a recognition that was signaled by the publication in 1899 of Eduard Bernstein's profoundly influential book *Evolutionary Socialism*. This recognition enabled the social democratic component of the socialist movement to attain significant political influence within several Western European nations during the course of the twentieth century and into the twenty-first, as well as within numerous other nations throughout the world. Ensuing sections of the essay return to world federalism. Some promising recent developments in world federalist thinking are noted, developments that may presage a revision of the world federalist goal away from the omnipotent world state, and toward some alternative form of limited world government that might be a more serious contender for actual implementation at some point within the foreseeable future. Parallels are observed between such a potential revision in world federalist thinking in the twenty-first century, and the actual revision in socialist thinking that occurred around the turn of the twentieth century. The salient practical distinctions between limited and unlimited world government are considered. The related issue of global economic inequality as an impediment to global political utility is taken up. The essay is concluded with a brief summary of the argument to be made that a properly designed limited federal world government would improve the human prospect over what it is likely to be if humanity continues onward indefinitely within the existing international political status quo.

A Brief History of World Government

The notion of a single political organization encompassing the whole of humanity—a world state—has intrigued mankind since earliest recorded history.[1] It is clear, however, that our contemporary idea of world government (formed peacefully through universal contract, purposes encompassing not only the preservation of peace but the general advancement of the human condition throughout the world) did not reach full fruition until the recent modern era. Well-known earlier proposals for a supernational political organization encompassing all the nations of the Earth, such as the Council of Ambassadors of the French monk Émeric Crucé, and the Congress of States of the German philosopher Immanuel Kant, were actually for no more than a universal mutual assistance alliance for the exclusive purpose of preserving peace.[2] The essence of these early concepts was eventually realized in the form of the League of Nations, established in 1919 immediately after World War I. The League was notably unsuccessful in its primary objective not only because of the non-adherence of the United States, but also because it had the misfortune of operating during what turned out to be an uneasy truce separating World Wars I and II. The successor organization to the League of Nations, the United Nations established in 1945 immediately after World War II, has also compiled an unimpressive peacekeeping record. Although it has indeed intervened successfully in a few cases of relatively minor regional conflicts, the UN was powerless against the Cold War confrontation between the communist and noncommunist blocs of nations that threatened a nuclear World War III. That such a horrific war did not erupt at some point during the perilous Cold War decades cannot reasonably be attributed to the existence and activities of the United Nations.

Prior to the mid-twentieth century, there had been numerous proposals for political organizations superior to the nation-states. Edith Wynner and Georgia Lloyd, world federalist activists of the 1930s and 1940s, compiled a large collection of such proposals.[3] Part II of their compilation ("There Is Nothing New under the Sun—Old Plans to Unite Nations Dating from 1306 to 1914,") briefly describes some 74 plans. Part III ("Theoretical Plans to Unite Nations since 1914") contains more detailed descriptions of an additional 25 plans (included in the categories "Universal" and "Federal" but not pertaining to the United Nations established in 1945) that were published between 1915 and 1944. However, a large proportion of these plans are for regional associations of relatively small subsets of nations, often amounting to little more than formalized military alliances. For example, many of the plans from the early modern era were motivated by the prospect that a tighter association among the Christian nations of Europe would enable more effective resistance against Muslim aggression, especially that emanating from the Ottoman empire.

It was the years just after World War II that saw the most intensive development of plans for world government in the current sense: plans that envisioned a full-fledged government organization encompassing all the nations of the world, with purposes confined not merely to peacekeeping, but extending also to overall human welfare-improvement by means beyond simply preventing wars. In other words, the current concept of world government involves a direct extrapolation of the manifold purposes of national governments toward their respective citizens, to the entire population of the world. Not that such plans were unknown prior to World War II. For example, during the World War I year of 1918, Raleigh C. Minor, a professor of constitutional and international law at the University of Virginia, published a treatise describing quite a modern concept of world government.[4] Although using the same name (League of Nations) as the real-world organization soon afterwards established by the Treaty of Versailles (1919), Minor's proposal was for something far more ambitious than the real-world League. Minor's League would have been a genuine world state with strong enforcement powers and democratic control by its citizens. Proposals analogous to that of Professor Minor became far more abundant following World War II.

The dramatic but highly ephemeral post-World War II "world government boom" is plausibly attributed to a shock reaction to the first (and thus far only) use of nuclear weapons in warfare, the August 1945 atomic bombings of Hiroshima and Nagasaki. This quantum leap in the destructiveness of weaponry lent more credence than ever before to the longstanding world federalist contention that the costs of war have become unendurable, and that the establishment of a strong world state is the only reliable means of avoiding these costs in the future. During the five years between the end of World War II in the summer of 1945 and the start of the Korean War in the summer of 1950, sympathetic interest in world government reached an unprecedented peak. An impassioned plea for world government (*The Anatomy of Peace* by Emery Reves) became an international bestseller, world-renowned intellectuals (Albert Einstein, Bertrand Russell, Robert Hutchins, and numerous others) declared their support for world government, world federalist organizations proliferated, and millions of people around the world began thinking seriously about the possibility.[5]

However, enthusiasm for world government subsided almost as quickly as it had arisen. It soon became apparent that the wartime alliance between the USSR and the Western powers had not abrogated the underlying ideological conflict between communism and noncommunism. The Soviet government still adhered to the orthodox Marxist doctrine that capitalism is doomed, and in reaction to this the people of the Western nations came to regard the USSR, especially now that it had progressed from being a wobbly infant in 1917 to a military colossus in 1945, as a dire threat to their accustomed way of life. Such events in 1949 as the communization of China and the first detonation of an atomic bomb by the Soviet Union, which ended the short-lived US nuclear monopoly, convinced many in the West that the communist leadership was seriously entertaining the possibility of a communist world empire within the relatively near future. As early as 1947, US president Harry Truman had proclaimed the "containment' doctrine: that further expansion of communism must be resisted by all means including military action, until such time as the communist leadership abandons its messianic aspirations.

As for fears of nuclear war, human beings are remarkably resilient and adaptive, mentally and emotionally as well as physically. Within a remarkably short space of time, most people had filed away the threat of dying in a worldwide nuclear holocaust in the same compartment as the threat of dying in an automobile accident. It was a regrettable but inevitable hazard, therefore there was nothing to be done about it. Furthermore, almost as soon as nuclear weapons became a part of reality, a general consensus arose, among the large majority of the population, that no one would be "stupid enough" to start a nuclear war. To some extent, this consensus, which is still prevalent today, may manifest wishful thinking. Among other things, a nuclear World War III could occur as a result of miscalculated brinkmanship, the same thing that was responsible for both World War I and World War II. Be that as it may, this consensus was (and remains) undeniably reassuring.

World federalists took a far less sanguine view of the nuclear war threat. In their view, the development of nuclear weapons immeasurably increased the overall threat to human civilization embodied in warfare. While the prospect of nuclear destruction might somewhat reduce the propensity toward provocative and belligerent behavior among nations, it would by no means eliminate it, and sooner or later some nation would stray over the line separating peace from unimaginably devastating warfare. What was obviously needed, in the view of world federalists, was something far stronger than the United Nations: what was needed was a genuine, fully functional world government with direct control over a large and dominant military force, with the power of taxation, and guided by officials subject to direct democratic accountability to the world population through free and open elections.

Although post-World War II world government proposals are highly diverse, most of them adhere in general terms to the 23 August 1947 declaration of the first World Congress of the World Movement for World Federal Government (WMWFG) held in Montreux, Switzerland. Taken together, the six points of the declaration are a prescription for a very centralized, powerful, and authoritative world state, for what is herein descriptively termed the "omnipotent world state." This became the common conception of world government at the time of the postwar world government boom, and it remains the common conception today. This conception was (and remains) simultaneously the world federalist ideal, and the bête noire of world government skeptics.

Contributions by postwar world federalists such as Giuseppe Borgese, Grenville Clark and Louis Sohn, and various others, that advocated the omnipotent world state, were summarily rejected by mainstream opinion.[6] As early as 1951, Gerard Mangone's comprehensive and influential treatise distilled the final postwar majority verdict on world government: a fine and noble idea in principle, but (alas) thoroughly impractical in the real world owing to the great strength of ideological preconceptions, cultural differences, and nationalistic prejudices. The basic problem, according to Mangone, is the absence of sufficient consensus within humanity on what constitutes a just and legitimate social order:[7]

> If a structure of world government is to be imagined, then its size, strength and shape will be conditioned by the social order it intends to establish. Should there be a genuine consensus among the members on the hierarchy of values within such a community, the coercive element will be minimized; if but little consensus exists, an autocratic leadership would be the obvious recourse for universal conformity.

The problem of "little consensus" was especially serious in the area of communist versus noncommunist ideology: disagreements over the relative merits of socialism versus capitalism, planning versus the market, Western-style democracy versus Party democracy, and so on. The negative verdict on world government enunciated by Mangone rapidly achieved consensus status among the vast majority of professional academics, political leaders, and rank-and-file citizens. On the other side of the ideological gap, communist ideologues were equally skeptical of world government. Just as Western analysts were leery of world government on grounds that it might be subverted and made into a tool of communist expansionism, so too communist ideologues were leery of world government on grounds that it might be subverted (from their point of view) and made into a tool of capitalist reaction.[8]

At the time, the end of the Cold War in the early 1990s could reasonably have been perceived as opening up new opportunities for world government. Throughout the Cold War, the first and foremost reason commonly cited for disregarding the possibility of world government had always been the ideological gap between the communist and noncommunist nations. But this specific impediment to world government, if not completely eliminated, was clearly less important. Just as the end of

World War I had seen the establishment of the League of Nations, and the end of World War II had seen the establishment of the stronger United Nations, it seemed to world federalists that perhaps the end of the Cold War might see a further advance toward an even stronger form of supernational organization, possibly even a legitimate, full-fledged, authoritative world government.

However, this did not happen. For one thing, World Wars I and II had been "hot" wars whereas the Cold War, as the term implies, was not. Although the threat of nuclear war had imposed a certain amount of psychic strain on humanity, this was not at all comparable to the prodigious amount of physical death, disability and destruction imposed on humanity by World Wars I and II. Furthermore, the collapse and dissolution of the Soviet Union had not totally abrogated the problem of ideology in the contemporary world. Most importantly, the People's Republic of China still maintains formal allegiance to communist principles, although it is apparently not currently interested in having these principles adopted by other nations. The continuing unrest in the Middle East, initiated back in 1948 by the creation of the Israel, which has been directly responsible for several wars in the region and indirectly responsible for numerous terrorist attacks both in the Mideast and throughout the world, including most horrifically 9/11, is to some extent exacerbated by religious doctrinal differences.

Last but not least, the economic gap between the richest First World nations and the poorest Third World nations continues to grow. Although the ideological impediment to world government has been markedly reduced by the subsidence of the Cold War, the economic impediment remains as significant as ever. People in the rich First World nations envision the possibility that an authoritative world government will decide to establish a global welfare state, by which the populations of the rich nations will be heavily taxed in order to provide welfare entitlements mostly benefiting the impoverished masses of the poor nations. Meanwhile, the poor nations are also apprehensive, envisioning the possibility that an authoritative world government will impose a global trade and investment regime that will essentially reestablish the exploitative relationships of the colonial era.

With these thoughts in mind, the contemporary mainstream consensus (the "conventional wisdom") is that even aside from the ideological issue, there is far too much heterogeneity in the world today for world government to be a viable proposition. In the hundreds of articles and dozens of books published every year in the popular and professional literature on contemporary international relations, terms such as "world government," "global government," "world state," and the like, rarely appear, and when they do, more often than not it is in the context of a cursory dismissal. The following typical example has been provided by the prominent contemporary authority on international relations, Anne-Marie Slaughter:[9]

> People and their governments around the world need global institutions to solve collective problems that can only be addressed on a global scale. They must be able to make and enforce global rules on a variety of subjects and through a variety of means... Yet world government is both infeasible and undesirable. The size and scope of such a government presents an unavoidable and dangerous threat to individual liberty. Further, the diversity of peoples to be governed makes it almost impossible to conceive of a global demos. No form of democracy within the current global repertoire seems capable of overcoming these obstacles.

A Brief History of Socialism

Although the modern history of socialism is commonly said to have commenced with the French Revolution of 1789, vague "socialistic" ideas (or ideals) of economic egalitarianism may of course be traced back to long before 1789. According to some sources, the term "socialism" itself was coined in 1832 by Pierre Leroux in the liberal French newspaper *Le Globe*. In its earliest and most general form, socialism was perceived as a means by which the adverse socioeconomic consequences of the Industrial Revolution, especially the poverty, misery and insecurity of the urban proletariat, could be ameliorated. Various avenues toward amelioration were envisioned. Some reformers, such as Charles Fourier, proposed the creation of relatively small, economically self-sufficient communes. Others, such as Robert Owen, proposed a sort of progressive capitalism by which the owners, perhaps under the authority of government regulators, would pay their workers generously and treat them fairly in the interest of higher productivity and greater workforce loyalty.

In their profoundly influential pamphlet *The Communist Manifesto* (1848), Karl Marx and Friedrich Engels dismissed these proposals as "utopian socialism." Fourier's ideas would not work because they ignored the economies of large-scale production only achievable through factory methods. Owen's ideas would not work because the capitalists were incapable of the sort of enlightened self-interest necessary to make them feasible. Marx and Engels' "scientific socialism," on the other hand, involved two core propositions: (1) fundamental reform of the modern industrial economy requires nothing less than the ownership of the capital means of production by society; (2) the only way this fundamental reform can be achieved is through violent revolution. Just as violent revolution had been necessary to the overthrow of the land-owning nobility by the industrial bourgeoisie, so too it would be necessary to the overthrow of the industrial bourgeoisie by the proletariat.

The Marx-Engels specification of socialism soon became dominant, to the point where the primary dictionary definition of "socialism" became (and remains today) "public ownership of capital." As the second half of the nineteenth century wore on, however, increasing doubt emerged even among committed Marxists. For one thing, intermittent efforts to achieve a socialist revolution, such as the Paris Commune of 1871, were notably unsuccessful. For another, the material condition of the working class seemed to be improving. It was becoming apparent that technological progress was enabling the improvement of general living conditions, while (perhaps) the threat of socialist revolution was persuading capitalists and political authorities to take advantage of these emerging economic opportunities. Toward the end of the nineteenth century, what we would today describe as the "social safety net" had taken hold throughout much of Western Europe and the world. Even such undemocratic nations as Imperial Germany, under the guidance of Chancellor Otto von Bismarck, were leading the way in certain areas, such as social insurance. In 1899, the ongoing reorientation of a substantial part of the socialist movement was dramatically manifested by the appearance of Bernstein's seminal contribution.

In that year, Eduard (sometimes Edward) Bernstein (1850-1932) published *Die Voraussetzungen des Sozialismus und die Aufgabe der Sozialdemokratie* (*The Preconditions of Socialism and the Tasks of Social Democracy*). In 1911, a somewhat abridged English translation by Edith C. Harvey was published by the New York publishing house B. W. Huebsch under the famous title *Evolutionary Socialism: A Criticism and Affirmation*.[10] In 1875, Bernstein had been one of the founders of the Sozialdemokratische Partei Deutschlands (SPD – Social Democratic Party of Germany), in which he remained active until his retirement in 1928. Based on a series of articles published in the party newspaper during the latter 1890s, his book explicitly rejected such fundamental tenets of conventional Marxist thought of the time as the inherent immorality and inefficiency of private ownership of land and capital, the inevitable immiseration of the proletariat, and the necessity for violent revolution to overthrow capitalism and inaugurate socialism. Bernstein argued that the condition of the working class was manifestly improving, that such reforms as business regulation, social insurance, and progressive taxation were effective means of achieving the underlying objectives of socialism, and that these reforms could and should be pursued through peaceful democratic means. From its initial appearance, his book was recognized as a major contribution to the theory and practice of socialism, eliciting both enthusiastic acclaim and furious denunciation.[11]

Among the denouncers was Vladimir Lenin, later to become famous as a prime mover of the successful Bolshevik revolution in Russia in 1917, and afterwards the first head of state of the newly established Union of Soviet Socialist Republics. To Lenin and like-minded critics such as SPD members Karl Kautsky, Karl Liebknecht and Rosa Luxemburg, revisionist socialism was a craven reformist sell-out of the traditional socialist vision, a sell-out that sought only "crumbs off the table" of the dominant class of capitalist plutocrats. To their minds, the only way to fully achieve the objectives of socialism was through socialism in the pure sense of public ownership and control of the means of production, and such a transformation could only come about by means of violent revolution. Although Marx's original view had been that the preconditions for revolution would eventually emerge through ever-worsening business depressions afflicting the industrially advanced capitalist nations, the vicissitudes imposed on the mainly agrarian Russian nation by World War I enabled Lenin's successful Bolshevik revolution in 1917 that established the USSR. But when Liebknecht and Luxemburg attempted an analogous revolution in defeated Germany in 1919, the revolution failed and its leaders were executed. This outcome seemed to vindicate the position of such centrists as Karl Kautsky that it would probably require a very long period of time to bring about conditions in the advanced capitalist nations under which socialist revolution would be successful.

Whether the Bolshevik revolution in Russia in fact contradicted Kautsky's position ultimately turns on the question of the degree of "success" attained through that revolution. The radical nature of Soviet communism, manifested by such policies as nationalization of agricultural land and industrial capital with little or no compensation paid to the former owners, and such actions as the execution of the Romanov royal family, elicited determined opposition from the outset. (Such policies might be compared to a rash attempt to establish the omnipotent world state in today's world.) Years of civil war and famine ensued. Although the Soviet Union recovered somewhat under the relatively moderate New Economic Plan of the 1920s, radical transformation was again pursued through the collectivization of agriculture and the crash industrialization program of the 1930s. Although impressive economic progress was achieved, the drastic internal stresses and strains imposed on the Soviet people by such policies were manifested by the consolidation of Joseph Stalin's dictatorial powers, comprehensive Party purges, mass executions, and the creation of the gulag archipelago of concentration camps to confine actual and suspected dissidents, and to extract slave labor from them under horrific conditions. Under Marxist leadership, the Soviet people then suffered, during the 1940s, through another world war, followed by more than four decades of a perilous Cold War confrontation with the bloc of noncommunist nations, a confrontation that threatened nuclear holocaust. To aggravate matters, the sluggish performance of the Soviet economy in the later stages of the Cold War was making a mockery of the leadership's promises to overtake the major Western nations in terms of per capita living standards. By the early 1990s, the Soviet people had finally had enough. The Marxist leadership was ousted and the Soviet Union was dissolved. (A peaceful political transformation of this magnitude had been almost unknown in prior human history—an extraordinary event that might hold out some hope that a federal world government, assuming it were properly designed, might be peacefully established at some point in the future.) Since then, its successor republics and erstwhile Eastern European satellites have been endeavoring to emulate the economic and political characteristics of the more successful Western nations. (In most cases, the emulation effort has not been easy.) In the very long run, therefore, covering the more than seven decades separating the Bolshevik revolution of 1917 from the dissolution of the USSR in 1991, it cannot be said that the revolution was a success.

Neither can success be plausibly attributed to such offshoots of Soviet communism as the People's Republic of China, Vietnam, North Korea, and Cuba. At the present time, the PRC is making dramatic economic progress, the result of abandoning Soviet-style central planning and strict egalitarianism, both of which were once considered fundamental to genuine socialism. But its political system remains fully oligarchic, fueling speculation that perhaps the contemporary Chinese model is incompatible with democracy as known elsewhere in the world. Aside from China, the economic and political performance of the handful of other nations in the contemporary world that continue to subscribe to communism is generally unimpressive.

Meanwhile, various key elements of social democracy as specified by Eduard Bernstein in *Evolutionary Socialism* have become integral parts of socioeconomic and political reality in all the most successful First World nations. Leaders of social democratic parties in these nations have taken an active part in governance throughout the twentieth century and into the twenty-first. For example, the German SPD was at times the largest political party in Germany (when not being suppressed by the Nazi government from 1933 through 1945), often participated in coalition governments, and remains today a major player in German politics.

Even "less progressive" nations such as the United States and Australia, which for the most part adamantly deny being tainted in any way by "socialism," are characterized by an abundance of business regulations, welfare programs, and progressive taxation. These elements of social democracy may be more advanced in other nations, especially in the Western European nations comprising the European Union, but this is arguably a matter of degree rather than of essence.

Of course, any real-world level of achievement falls short of the imaginable ideal. Even in those nations that proudly advertise themselves as "socialist" in the social democratic sense, retention of private ownership of most of the means of production under modern conditions (domination of economic production by large corporations, separation of ownership and control, important role of institutional investors, and so on) results in highly unequal distribution of capital property income, a category of income that has the appearance of being unearned. Aside from that, there are other continuing problems with the existing system (whether it be deemed "capitalist" or "socialist"): recurrent business recessions, persistent unemployment, speculative bubbles, and so on—though many of these may be the necessary concomitants of any market system, whether it be market capitalist or (in the case of the PRC) market socialist. It is held by some idealists that until all these kinds of shortcomings are completely eliminated, society cannot be described as "genuinely socialist." If this viewpoint were accepted, then nothing short of utopia would be genuinely socialist.

The success or failure of a socioeconomic system is necessarily evaluated in terms of some basis. If we compare nations such as the United States, Britain, France and Germany, to name a few, as they were in the year 2000 relative to what they were in the year 1900, only the most contrarian mentalities would be unwilling to acknowledge significant progress. Living standards are higher, equality is higher, and democratic influence on the government is higher. Not that there was a linear trend of progress throughout the twentieth century. During the tumultuous decades of the first half of the twentieth century, the nations of Western Europe suffered through economic depression, fascist dictatorships, and devastating warfare. But during the second half of the twentieth century, Western Europe sailed through calmer waters. Among the reasons for its long-run success would appear to be the renunciation of the orthodox Marxist doctrine of pure public ownership socialism through violent revolution, and its replacement by the revisionist Marxist doctrine of virtual socialism through peaceful evolution.

What, if anything, does the above-described historical development within the socialist movement imply about the potential future development of the world federalist movement? There are two salient questions to be addressed: (1) whether an analogous renunciation might be possible within the world federalist movement away from the omnipotent world state concept and toward a limited federal world government concept, and (2) if so, whether such a renunciation would strengthen the world federalist movement and enhance the prospects that a real-world federal world government might be achieved within the foreseeable future. Prior to addressing these central questions, it will be useful to consider certain recent trends in world federalist thought that might be promising indicators, and to specify in more detail what is implied, in a practical sense, by a the notion of "limited" federal world government.

Recent Developments in World Federalist Thought

Despite the continued prevalence of the conventional wisdom on world government well exemplified by the above quotation from Anne-Marie Slaughter's *A New World Order*, the historian Campbell Craig has written of a recent "resurgence" of interest in world government.[12] What evidence is there for this alleged resurgence? To begin with, during the mid-2000s, perhaps in response to the traumatic 9/11 event, there may have been a spike in the production of appeals for world government from world federalist enthusiasts whose strident "one world or none" message harks back to the 1945-50 world government boom.[13] Of course, if appeals of this nature went unheeded during the perilous decades of the Cold War, they are even less likely to be effective now that the Cold War is history and the threat of nuclear world war in the near future has greatly receded.

What may be more significant is that a trickle has apparently begun of more restrained and scholarly world government advocacies from authors with reputable academic credentials.[14] While these more reflective and balanced advocacies are more likely to elicit serious interest in world government among those who are currently skeptical of the concept, the fact remains that they are still very few in number. Moreover, they are generally somewhat vague on the institutional specifics of the world government being advocated. Advocacies that focus on the various potential benefits of world government while paying insufficient attention to the potential costs, specifically to the danger that an omnipotent world state, of the sort envisioned in conventional world federalist thought, might soon degenerate into totalitarian tyranny, are unlikely to be taken seriously.

A major focus in Craig's "resurgence" article is on a very unusual article by the eminent international relations authority Alexander Wendt, provocatively entitled "Why a World State Is Inevitable" (2003).[15] Inasmuch as the question of inevitability is only sensibly considered with reference to existent reality, and as world government is not yet part of existent reality, Wendt's proposition is clearly not meant to be taken literally. Rather it is deliberately provocative: intended merely to elicit additional serious thought about the world government possibility. Wendt's inevitability essay has indeed been cited in a substantial number of contributions to the professional literature.

But whether this attention will lead to a serious challenge to the existing strong consensus against world government remains to be seen. While most of the contributions that cite Wendt's article seem at least somewhat sympathetic toward world government, none of them significantly amplifies or expands Wendt's argument. In fact, thus far the only full-scale engagement with Wendt's "inevitability thesis" has been a critical commentary by Vaughn Shannon (2005).[16] Many of the citations fall into the "see also" category. Eric Posner (2006) points out the lack of immediate relevance of the thesis: "Wendt is in a very small minority, and as he puts off the creation of world government for at least another century, the possibility has no relevant short-term implications even if he is correct"; while Thomas G. Weiss (2009) suggests that there is nothing especially innovative about the thesis: "From time to time a contemporary international relations theorist, like Alexander Wendt, suggests that 'a world state is inevitable' (Wendt 2003, 2005; Shannon 2005), or Daniel Deudney (2006) wishes one were because war has become too dangerous."[17] If indeed the inevitability thesis is eventually recognized as a serious challenge to the mainstream consensus against world government, quite possibly the outcome will simply be a further refining and strengthening of the conventional case against world government that underpins the current consensus.

In support of his argument that a world state is, as alleged in the title of his article, "inevitable," Alexander Wendt marshals an argument based upon teleological reasoning, According to teleological reasoning, everything in the universe has a purpose toward which it inevitably tends. Just as human babies tend to fulfill their purpose by developing into human adults, so too global human civilization is tending toward its final purpose: a global state. The argument is clever and fleshed out impressively with facts and concepts derived from a wide range of human knowledge. As a piece of erudite writing, Wendt's article is quite impressive. But it is more likely to be persuasive to a theoretical philosopher than to the typical international relations professional, let alone to the typical international relations practitioner or the typical member of the general public.

Be that as it may, Wendt offers skeptical readers of his inevitability essay two pieces of reasonably solid practical evidence that a world state will eventually be established: (1) the very long-run historical trend toward greater and greater political consolidation that has brought humanity from the tens of thousands of small, autonomous tribal units of prehistory down to the 200-odd nation-states of today, several of which encompass populations in the tens and even hundreds of millions; (2) the fact that a world state would benefit both large nations (lower probability of debilitating wars with other large nations) and small nations (lower probability of being subjected to the oppressive hegemony of large nations). Both of these points are significant and worthy of consideration, but in and of themselves, they are far from conclusive.

With respect to the long-term trend toward ever greater political consolidation, the hard fact remains that almost all of this consolidation was brought about, in one way or another, by means of warfare. In the nuclear age, it seems unlikely that additional warfare offers a plausible avenue toward further political consolidation leading to a world state. One must also consider the fact that there has been a considerable amount of political deconsolidation in the recent past, ranging from the dissolution of the great European colonial empires to the disintegration of the Soviet Union and Yugoslavia.

With respect to the potential benefits of world government for both the large nations and the small nations, it must be acknowledged that these are definite potential benefits, and need to be taken into account in any sensible evaluation of the world government possibility. But potential benefits have to be weighed against potential costs. The contemporary consensus is that the potential costs of world government (totalitarian tyranny, bureaucratic suffocation, cultural homogenization, global civil war) far exceed the potential benefits. Simply enumerating benefits, while paying little or no attention to costs, is unlikely to be rhetorically effective, given that the costs are so widely accepted.

Although there are obvious difficulties with Professor Wendt's "inevitability of world government" thesis, the fact that the author is a recognized and respected international relations authority, and the fact that his article was published in a reputable, mainstream international relations periodical, are quite significant facts. It is not too much to suggest that 30 years ago, with the Cold War still raging, no recognized and respected international relations authority would have dreamed of writing such an article, and no reputable, mainstream international relations periodical would have dreamed of publishing it. Therefore, the appearance of this article, in and of itself, may be a significant indicator of increased receptivity toward the concept of world government, at least among academic professionals in the international relations discipline. In due course, increased receptivity among the attentive elite may lead to increased receptivity among the intelligentsia generally, the general public, and the political leadership.

Also highly relevant for our present purposes is that within his influential article, Professor Wendt suggests that the putatively "inevitable" world state he has in mind might well be something quite different from the traditional world federalist ideal of the omnipotent world state:

> Lest I be accused of lacking imagination, however, it should be emphasized that the systemic changes needed for a world state could be fulfilled in various ways, and so a world state might look very different than states today. In particular, it could be much more decentralized, in three respects. First, it would not require its elements to give up local autonomy. Collectivizing organized violence does not mean that culture, economy or local politics must be collectivized; subsidiarity could be the operative principle. Second, it would not require a single UN army. As long as a structure exists that can command and enforce a collective response to threats, a world state could be compatible with the existence of national armies, to which enforcement operations might be sub-contracted (along the lines of NATO perhaps). Finally, it would not even require a world "government", if by this we mean a unitary body with one leader whose decisions are final… As long as binding choices can be made, decision-making in a world state could involve broad deliberation in a "strong" public sphere rather than command by one person.

It is the position of the present author that in a practical sense, no world state is inevitable, and this holds especially for the omnipotent world state. However, on the spectrum of possibility over the foreseeable future, limited world government is far more likely than unlimited world government.

Limited versus Unlimited World Government

Perhaps what will eventually be perceived as the single most significant post-Cold War challenge to the conventional wisdom on world government is simply increased awareness, among both world government skeptics and world government supporters, that there might exist viable world government possibilities that would go well beyond the existent United Nations, but would stop well short of the traditional world federalist ideal of the omnipotent world state. Just as Eduard Bernstein made social democracy a politically viable movement throughout the twentieth century through his development of "evolutionary socialism," possibly world federalism will become a politically viable movement in the twenty-first century through the development of "evolutionary world government." According to Bernstein's redefinition, "socialism" need not involve public ownership of all or most of the stock of nonhuman factors of production. It goals can be achieved to a reasonable level of fulfillment by means other than public ownership of capital: by means such as progressive taxation, social welfare programs, and business regulation. Consequently, in this more widely acceptable form—a "kinder, gentler socialism"— it need not be achieved by means of violent revolution.

An analogous redefinition of a "kinder, gentler world government" would dispense with such requirements as universal membership, prohibition of withdrawal from the world federation of member nations, and monopolization by the world federation of all heavy weaponry. If potential member nations in a world government do not expect to be disarmed as a consequence of taking membership, and if they are allowed freedom to depart the federation if at some future time they so desire, resistance to the idea of world government would likely be significantly diminished. Most people today are opposed to world government—even though they will readily grant that such a government would be, at a minimum, a reliable guarantor against nuclear holocaust—because they fear that a militarily all-powerful world government would undertake policies that would be highly detrimental to their own nation, and to themselves personally, and there would be no means available to their nation for "opting out" of the world federation. Their nation would be "trapped" within a hostile and dysfunctional political structure. A constitutional promise to the member nations of the right of free exit from the world state if they so desire— and of independent control over sufficient military force to back up this right effectively—would reassure the people of potential member nations that a means of escape would be available if needed. These rights would play the same role as putting fire escapes on buildings, and of equipping ships with lifeboats. The hope is that these safeguards will never be needed—but if the need does arise, they are available.

The obvious question presents itself, however, whether a government that shares military power with its subsidiary components, and that allows the departure of subsidiary components at their own unilateral discretion, can be considered a legitimate state. Certainly these provisions are incompatible with the common conception of statehood at the national level. For example, the United States does not permit the state governments to exercise independent control of military forces (as opposed to police forces) stationed within their borders, and the US Civil War of 1861-1865 manifested the determination of the national government to maintain the integrity of the union against secession efforts by some of the component states. Be that as it may, however, the common conception of statehood at the national level is not necessarily the only legitimate conception of statehood. The power and authority of a given state entity might lie anywhere along a wide spectrum from weakest to strongest. As long as power and authority is not totally absent, the entity may arguably be deemed a legitimate state.[18]

Probably the most comprehensive and detailed blueprint for a limited federal world government currently available in the international relations literature is the proposal for a Federal Union of Democratic Nations of James A. Yunker.[19] Although the word "democratic" is included in the name of the proposed federation, it is emphasized that the only requirement for membership would be the *intention* to establish fully democratic institutions, for those nations in which such institutions do not currently exist, once their citizen bodies have been properly prepared for their responsibilities under the democratic form of government. No time frame would be specified for such preparation. The practical purpose of this provision, of course, is to make available membership to various nations that are not presently fully democratic in the generally accepted sense, the prime example of this being the People's Republic of China.

The proposed Federal Union would be a full-fledged government entity, composed of legislative, executive and judicial branches, the high officials of which would be directly elected by the populations of the member nations. It would be constitutionally based, would possess the authority to levy taxes, and would directly control an armed force roughly comparable to the armed force of one of the smaller nuclear powers such as the UK. It would possess the ordinary trappings and emblems of state authority: flag, anthem, capital city, permanent administrative apparatus, and so on. On the other hand, it would operate under the critical constraints mentioned above: member nations would be free to depart the federation at their own unilateral discretion, and member nations would also retain independent control over as much military force as desired, even including strategic nuclear weapons.

Another important safeguard against possible tendencies toward unacceptable policy directions would be adoption of a "dual voting system" in the federation legislature. Proposed legislation would have to be approved by a majority on two different bases: the population basis and the material basis. In the population vote, the weight given to the vote of each particular representative would be proportional to the population of the district represented, relative to the total population of the federation.

In the material vote, the weight given to the vote of each representative would be proportional to the financial revenues derived from the district represented, relative to the total financial revenues of the federation. Representatives from the rich nations would be disproportionately represented in the material vote, while representatives from populous poorer nations would be disproportionately represented in the population vote. Since measures would have to be approved on both the material basis and the population basis, only measures on which rich nations and poor nations could achieve reasonable consensus would be approved by the federation legislature. The dual voting system is designed to preclude the passage of any legislation that would be unacceptable to either the First World nations or the Third World nations. Prime examples would be legislation aimed at a drastic redistribution of current world income by means of a global welfare state (which would be opposed by the rich nations), and legislation that might be deemed an effort to reestablish conditions of colonial exploitation (which would be opposed by the poor nations).

Obviously the proposed dual voting system is inconsistent with the ideal of pure democracy, wherein each citizen of the polity exercises one and only one vote. This is a third major departure, along with free exit and independent national military forces, from the conventional world federalist concept. In an ideal world in which all nations had comparable living standards, this departure from the one-person-one-vote principle would not be necessary. But it is important to recognize that the practical relevance of the distinction between the population vote and the material vote would be eliminated were all nations of the world to have approximately equal per capita income. In that case, the revenues raised from each district would tend to be basically proportional to the district's population.

Prospects for Global Economic Equality

A condition under which the results from the population vote would be identical to the results from the material vote is the long-term objective of Yunker's complementary economic proposal for a World Economic Equalization Program, in effect a Global Marshall Plan. Since he is an economist by profession, it is understandable that Yunker's political proposal for a Federal Union of Democratic Nations is closely linked to his proposal for a greatly expanded, worldwide economic development assistance program. The idea of greatly reducing, or even altogether eliminating, the world poverty problem, through the global equivalent of the

Marshall Plan that facilitated the rebuilding process in Europe following World War II, has long been a staple of visionary thought, and is continuing notably at the present time in the activities of the Global Marshall Plan Initiative, a pressure group primarily active in Europe.[20]

Against the currently prevalent opinion that an increase in the level of foreign development assistance would have little impact on global economic inequality (since the aid resources would be diverted and/or misallocated), Yunker has adduced evidence derived from computer simulation of a model of the world economy to the effect that, despite the very formidable size of the current economic gap, it could in fact be overcome within a relatively brief period of historical time, something on the order of 50 years, by a sufficiently massive and coördinated economic development assistance effort.[21] The benchmark simulation results suggest that a dramatic acceleration in the rate of growth of living standards in the poor nations could be achieved at the very minor cost of a slight retardation in the rate of growth of living standards in the rich nations. The cost to the rich nations would not be a decline in their living standards, nor even a noticeable decline in the rate of growth of their living standards. In other words, the material cost to the people of the rich nations would be very minor. The author concedes, however, that these positive results are obtained using benchmark parameter values that might be too optimistic. Sensitivity analyses using sufficiently adverse values of certain critical model parameters demonstrate that the outcome could be just as pessimists would predict: despite huge investments, very little improvement in average living standards within the recipient nations. Therefore the results of these computer simulations *do not prove* that the outcome from a Global Marshall Plan would be favorable. However, they do *demonstrate the possibility* that the outcome would be favorable.

Yunker's argument is not that world government and a Global Marshall Plan would assuredly be successful. These initiatives should be regarded as experiments, experiments which may or may not be successful. The currently available evidence is inconclusive, because these experiments have not thus far been undertaken. Unless we actually undertake such experiments, we cannot know how they will turn out. If, after a reasonable period of time, it is becoming compellingly evident that they are not working, then the Global Marshall Plan could be shut down and the world federation disbanded. There is a workable "exit strategy," so to speak. Even in the event of failure, however, no doubt some lessons will have been learned that will be useful to the future development of global human civilization.

Perhaps the most potent argument against world government at the present time is that if such a government were to be established, there would be no way to return to the status quo ante short of violent revolution. Were this argument to be widely recognized as specious, this might significantly improve the odds that an actual world government will be established in the real world within the foreseeable future. It has long been acknowledged that the main basis of progress in physical science is experimentation. Clearly there might be a role for experiment in social policy. The repeal of alcohol prohibition in the United States in 1933, and the renunciation of communism by the Soviet Union in 1991, are two examples of a society "changing its mind" on the basis of experience ("experience" being a form of "experiment"). What happened to alcohol prohibition in the United States and communism in the Soviet Union might also happen to a world government in the future. Nevertheless, it will be agreed by most policy analysts that the large majority of social and political innovations that come about in the real world, against much opposition and with great difficulty, are eventually recognized by the large majority as having been generally beneficial, and thus they become permanent.

The vision of world government as a probable catalyst to global civil war is so firmly imbedded in most people's minds that it might seem implausible that following the formation of a global government, that government would permit the peaceful departure of component nations—whether or not this is a constitutionally guaranteed national right. The example of the United States Civil War of 1861 to 1865 is likely to be invoked: the US national government, supported by the northern states, undertook a long and costly civil war rather than allow the peaceful secession of the southern states. But aside from the fact that the US Constitution that went into effect in 1789 did not address the issue of secession, either to allow it or disallow it, the question of slavery introduced an extremely emotional element into the situation, an element that made it impossible for either the northern states or the southern states to give in and allow a peaceful compromise. As we look toward the future, it hard to imagine an issue confronting the world government that would be so combustible as was the issue of slavery in the United States in 1861. To assume that such issues must necessarily arise may be unduly pessimistic.

The Case for (Limited) Federal World Government

It was during the hyper-violent twentieth century, with its two world wars and the threat of a nuclear third world war, that the world federalist concept of a world state to ensure world peace came to full fruition. But just as the case for world government came into sharper focus during the twentieth century, so also did the case against world government. The two most important arguments against world government are: first, that it would quickly degenerate into a horrific totalitarian nightmare, as in Kenneth Waltz: "And were world government attempted, we might find ourselves dying in the attempt, or uniting and living a life worse than death."[22]; and second, that there is no need for world government because the intelligence and good sense of national leaders will keep nations from going to war with one another, as in the "anarchical society" of Hedley Bull.[23] For obvious reasons, the second argument is hardly mentioned when wars are currently in progress, as in 1914-1918 or 1939-1945. But in peacetime it flourishes, to an ever-greater degree as the peaceful interlude lengthens.

This second argument is nowadays frequently enunciated using the vocabulary of "global governance." In the early 1990s, following the collapse and dissolution of the Soviet Union, the idea arose and developed that now that the ideological problem had greatly diminished, international cooperation through the United Nations and other trans-national organizations could advance to such a high level that the results would be comparable to what would be achieved if there were an actual world government in operation. This idea has since been explored in numerous contributions in the IR literature.[24] In its neutral sense, "global governance" simply refers to the existent degree of international cooperation, whether that degree be high or low. But according to most dictionaries, "governance" is what governments do, so that the phrase "governance without government" (utilized as the title of the seminal 1992 contribution of Rosenau and Czempiel) is in a strict sense an oxymoron.[25] In fact, it may be a form of wishful thinking to utilize the term "global governance" to describe and characterize the current international regime.

Despite the ebbing of the Cold War 20 years ago, the military superpowers still feel it necessary to maintain large armed forces equipped with nuclear weapons. Some small, non-nuclear nations ("rogue" nations) are endlessly fascinated by the prospect of acquiring such weapons, as are terrorist groups desirous of surpassing the 9/11 success of Al-Qaeda. This situation elicits concern over such questions, for example, as just how far the other nuclear powers will allow the United States and its allies to go in quest of security against nuclear proliferation and nuclear terrorism. Leaving aside apocalyptic visions, localized conflict situations (as in Rwanda, Bosnia, Darfur and elsewhere) continue to produce much human misery, the population explosion throughout the world over the last century is putting ever-greater pressure on both the natural resource base and the purity of the natural environment, and the AIDS crisis has reminded us of our potential vulnerability to catastrophic epidemics of contagious diseases. These are global problems in that they have important ramifications in almost every nation on the planet. The extent to which humanity will be able to cope effectively with these problems is critically affected by the predisposition among nations toward mutual respect, trust and cooperation. The persistence of us-versus-them attitudes in the various national populations makes it more difficult for national governments to reach effective, binding agreements on global problems.

If there existed in the real world the world federalist ideal of the omnipotent world state, clearly there would then be little or no possibility of a nuclear holocaust, and it also seems likely that dramatic progress would be assured toward the amelioration of other global hazards such as environmental deterioration. But despite these advantages of the omnipotent world state, which have been virtually self-evident for many decades, the possibility has been thoroughly rejected by the overwhelming majority of the human population of the world, for fear of totalitarian tyranny, bureaucratic suffocation, cultural homogenization, and so on. Common sense would seem to dictate that the possibility of establishing an omnipotent world state in the real world within the foreseeable future is negligible to non-existent.

According to the ancient proverb, "half a loaf is better than none." What may be possible in the real world within the foreseeable future is the establishment of a limited federal world government along the lines of the Federal Union of Democratic Nations described above. Clearly the establishment of such a limited world government, even if it were accompanied by the initiation of a Global Marshall Plan, would not immediately abrogate the problems of the world. It seems likely that at the outset membership would not be universal, and moreover, even among the charter members, some nations would retain virtually the same military machines they possess now. This is especially true of military superpowers such as the United States, the Russian Federation, and the People's Republic of China. The possibility of nuclear world war would not be eliminated, and in the very short run it might not even be noticeably reduced. Furthermore, even with a massive Global Marshall Plan in operation, it would almost certainly require several decades to achieve a condition in which the economic differences between First World and Third World nations would be insignificant. Until such time as a high level of economic equality is achieved throughout the world, economic differences will continue to generate conflicts of interest between rich and poor nations, conflicts that will continue to impede effective global action against such long-term threats as natural resource depletion and environmental deterioration.

But the fact that global perfection would not be instantaneously achieved is not a sensible argument against proposals for a limited world government and a Global Marshall Plan. The appropriate comparison is between the status quo as it exists now, and the probable situation were these possibilities to be implemented. A plausible case can be made that the global human condition would be better were these initiatives undertaken. There would be some improvement in the processes of global governance in the short run, but more importantly, a more secure basis would have been laid for accelerating improvement in these processes in the long run.

An existing, functioning world government would provide a focus for the furtherance of impulses within national governments toward international cooperation, and for the deepening of cosmopolitan tendencies within the global human population. Many people today, not just world federalists, believe that it would be a good thing if people everywhere thought of themselves as "citizens of the world." The problem with this is that the condition of citizenship implies a political entity of which one is a part, and to which one owes allegiance. But "the world" as presently constituted is not a political entity. It is difficult to experience allegiance toward a planetary body, or even to the collectivity of humanity residing on that planetary body—when most of those people are citizens of other nations whose interests are often perceived to be in conflict with one's own interests. Whereas the phrase "citizen of the world" is an unpersuasive abstraction, the phrase "citizen of the world federation" would possess practical significance. In other words, while the notion of patriotism toward "the world" is meaningless and nonsensical, the notion of patriotism toward "the world federation" is meaningful and sensible.

The existence of a formal world government, even though relatively weak at first, would tend to support a growing sense of world community, and strengthening world community would enable a stronger and more effective world government, which in turn would further strengthen the spirit of world community, and so on. A snowballing effect could be set in motion, leading eventually to a very strong sense of world community, and a commensurately authoritative and effective world government. Such reserved national rights as free exit and independent military forces, rights required to permit the foundation of the world government in today's nationally oriented world, would at that point in time be no more than dimly remembered historical relics. Thus the concept of "evolutionary world government" might underpin a successful world federalist movement in the twenty-first century, in much the same way that Eduard Bernstein's concept of "evolutionary socialism" enabled the success of the social democratic movement throughout most of the world in the twentieth century.

Notes

1. According to Derek Heater's authoritative history, *World Citizenship and Government: Cosmopolitan Ideas in the History of Western Political Thought* (New York: St. Martin's Press, 1996), the conceptual roots of the notion of world government may be traced back to the ancient Greeks.

2. Émeric Crucé's *The New Cyneas* was originally published in French in 1623. Its English translation by Thomas Willing Balch was published under the title *The New Cyneas of Émeric Crucé* (Philadelphia: Allan, Lane and Scott, 1909). The 1909 edition was reprinted by Kessinger Publishing in 2010. Originally published in German in 1795, Immanuel Kant's *Perpetual Peace: A Philosophical Essay* was translated into English by Mary Campbell Smith (London: Swan Sonnenschein & Co., 1903). The 1903 edition was reprinted by Cosimo Classics in 2005.

3. Edith Wynner and Georgia Lloyd, *Searchlight on Peace Plans: Choose Your Road to World Government* (New York: E. P. Dutton, 1944).

4. Raleigh C. Minor, *A Republic of Nations: A Study of the Organization of a Federal League of Nations* (New York: Oxford University Press, 1918).

5. Emery Reves, *The Anatomy of Peace*, second edition (New York: Harper and Brothers, 1945). For accounts of the period, see Joseph P. Baratta, *The Politics of World Federation*, Vol. I: *United Nations, UN Reform, Atomic Control*, Vol. II: *From World Federalism to Global Governance* (Westport, Conn.: Praeger, 2004), and James A. Yunker, *The Idea of World Government: From Ancient Times to the Twenty-First Century* (London and New York: Routledge Global Institutions Series, 2011).

6. Giuseppe A. Borgese, *Foundations of the World Republic.* (Chicago: University of Chicago Press, 1953). Borgese's volume included as an appendix the "Preliminary Draft of a World Constitution" that had been developed in the immediate post-World War II by a committee of distinguished citizens chaired by Robert M. Hutchins, at that time president of the University of Chicago. Grenville Clark and Louis B. Sohn, *World Peace through World Law*, third enlarged edition (Cambridge, Mass: Harvard University Press, 1966). The Clark-Sohn volume took the form of an annotated revision of the existing United Nations Charter.

7. Gerald J. Mangone, *The Idea and Practice of World Government* (New York: Columbia University Press, 1951), p. 19.

8. Eliot R. Goodman, *The Soviet Design for a World State* (New York: Columbia University Press, 1960), pp. 396 ff.

9. Anne-Marie Slaughter, *A New World Order* (Princeton: Princeton University Press, 2004), p. 8.

10. Edward Bernstein, *Evolutionary Socialism: A Criticism and Affirmation.* Originally published in German in 1899. Translated by Edith C. Harvey (New York: B. W. Huebsch, 1911). Reprinted by Random House in 1961 and Kessinger Publishing in 2009.

11. Illustrative of the substantial literature on this pivotal development in the history of socialist thought are the following: Peter Gay, *The Dilemma of Democratic Socialism: Eduard Bernstein's Challenge to Marx* (New York: Octagon Books, 1979); David McLellan, *Marxism after Marx: An Introduction* (New York: Harper and Row, 1979); J. M. Tudor, ed., *Marxism and Social Democracy: The Revisionist Debate, 1896-1898* (New York: Cambridge University Press, 1988); Manfred B. Steger, *Eduard Bernstein and the Quest for Evolutionary Socialism* (New York: Cambridge University Press, 1997).

12. Campbell Craig, "The Resurgent Idea of World Government," *Ethics & International Affairs* 22(2): 133-142, Summer 2008.

13. Examples include Jerry Tetalman and Byron Belitsos, *One World Democracy: A Progressive Vision for Enforceable World Law* (San Rafael, California: Origin Press, 2005); Errol E. Harris, *Earth Federation Now: Tomorrow Is Too Late* (Radford, Virginia: Institute for Economic Democracy, 2005); Jim Clark, *Rescue Plan for Planet Earth: Democratic World Government through a Global Referendum* (Toronto: Key Publishing, 2008).

14. Examples include Luis Cabrera *Political Theory of Global Justice: A Cosmopolitan Case for the World State* (New York: Routledge, 2004); Louis Pojman, *Terrorism, Human Rights, and the Case for World Government* (Lanham, Md.: Rowman & Littlefield, 2006); Torbjörn Tännsjö, *Global Democracy: The Case for a World Government* (Edinburgh: Edinburgh University Press, 2008).

15. Alexander Wendt, "Why a World State Is Inevitable," *European Journal of International Relations* 9(4): 491-542, October 2003.

16. Vaughn P. Shannon, "Wendt's Violation of the Constructivist Project: Agency and Why a World State is *Not* Inevitable," *European Journal of International Relations* 11(4): 581-587, October 2005. Wendt's response is contained in "Agency, Teleology, and the World State: A Reply to Shannon," *European Journal of International Relations* 11(4): 589-598, October 2005.

17. Eric A. Posner, "International Law: A Welfarist Approach," *University of Chicago Law Review* 73(2): 487-543, Spring 2006. Thomas G. Weiss, "What Happened to the Idea of World Government," *International Studies Quarterly* 53(2): 253-271, June 2009.

18. See, for example, recent work on "governance in areas of limited statehood": Thomas Risse and Ursula Lehmkuhl, "Governance in Areas of Limited

Statehood: New Modes of Governance," SFB-Governance Working Paper 1, December 2006; Tanja A. Börzel and Thomas Risse, "Governance without a State: Can It Work?" *Regulation and Governance* 4(2): 113-134, June 2010. Also relevant is the abundant literature on the mixed political nature of the European Union: examples include Jeremy J. Richardson, ed., *European Union: Power and Policy-Making* (New York: Routledge, 1997); Richard McAllister, *From EC to EU: An Historical and Political Survey* (New York: Routledge, 1997); Clive Archer, *The European Union* (New York: Routledge, 2008).

19. James A. Yunker, *Political Globalization: A New Vision of Federal World Government* (Lanham, Md.: University Press of America, 2007); *The Grand Convergence: Economic and Political Aspects of Human Progress* (New York: Palgrave Macmillan, 2010).

20. Franz Josef Rademacher, *Global Marshal Plan: A Planetary Contract* (Hamburg, Germany: Global Marshall Plan Foundation, 2004); Florian J. Huber, *Global Governance and the Global Marshall Plan* (Saarbrücken, Germany: Verlag Publishing, 2007); Andreas Pichlhöfer, *World in Balance – Global Marshall Plan* (Saarbrücken, Germany: Verlag Publishing, 2010).

21. James A. Yunker, *Common Progress: The Case for a World Economic Equalization Program* (New York: Praeger, 2000), "Could a Global Marshall Plan Be Successful? An Investigation Using the WEEP Simulation Model," *World Development* 32(7): 1109-1137, July 2004.

22. Kenneth N. Waltz, *Man, the State and War* (New York: Columbia University Press, 1959), p. 228.

23. Hedley Bull, *The Anarchical Society: A Study of Order in World Politics* (New York: Columbia University Press, 1977).

24. Illustrative references from the abundant literature on global governance include the following: Albert J. Paolini, Anthony P. Jarvis, and Christian Reus-Smit, eds., *Between Sovereignty and Global Governance: The United Nations, the State and Civil Society* (New York: St. Martin's Press, 1998); Martin Hewson and Timothy J. Sinclair, eds., *Approaches to Global Governance Theory* (Albany, NY: State University of New York Press, 1999); Rorden Wilkinson and Stephen Hughes, eds., *Global Governance: Critical Perspectives* (New York: Routledge, 2002).

25. James N. Rosenau and Ernst-Otto Czempiel, eds., *Governance without Government: Order and Change in World Politics* (Cambridge: Cambridge University Press, 1992).

4

From National Sovereignty to Global Government: Is There a Plausible Transition Path?

As someone who believes firmly that world government is both feasible and desirable within the foreseeable future, I personally would most certainly answer in the affirmative the question posed in the title of this essay. But there is a difference between a plausible transition path to global government *existing*, and that plausible transition path *being discovered and taken* by humanity. To illustrate, there might in reality exist a feasible path that could be taken to the top of a high mountain, but that fact does not guarantee that the path will actually be discovered and utilized by mountain climbers. If mountain climbers believe firmly that no climbable path exists to the top of some particular mountain, they will stop looking for it. And of course if they are not looking for it, they will not find it.

My own personal epiphany that a properly designed world government would be beneficial occurred when I was a young man during the turbulent 1960s. Since then I have done as much as I could toward spreading awareness of this fact among whomever I could reach either via the spoken word or the printed word. But having run up against a brick wall of skepticism and indifference over the years and decades, my youthful enthusiasm and optimism is now much diminished. It is not that a path to the top of the mountain does not exist; it is rather that the likelihood of the path being discovered within the foreseeable future is depressingly low. I have not given up by any means, and I fully intend to continue my efforts for as long as I am physically able to. But my subjective estimate of the probability that my generation will live long enough to witness the formation of a world government is gradually sinking lower and lower.

Be that as it may, I do believe that there are certain things that might be done by the tiny minority of world federalists to increase the likelihood that the path will indeed—despite the odds—be discovered, and it is my intention in this essay to share these ideas with my fellow world federalists. Some of what I have to say may be somewhat offensive to some of my fellow believers in the world government goal. I believe that mistakes have been made in the past, and that these same mistakes are continuing to be made in the present—mistakes serious enough to drastically diminish the probability that the world government goal will be achieved within the lifetimes of anyone now alive. But in my view these mistakes are rectifiable. If such rectification takes place, the world federalist movement will become far more effective and influential than it has been in the past, and unmistakable, dramatic progress will start being made toward the goal that we all cherish—a benign and effective world government. Certainly what I propose in the following would require many if not most world federalists to alter their current mindsets. We all know how difficult it is to alter a long-established mindset. But in some cases, such alteration might make the difference between endless, frustrating failure, and the beginning of progress toward genuine success.

A Pragmatic Plan toward World Government

At the present time, an extremely strong consensus exists within the human race that any sort of a meaningful world state would be totally impractical. Either such a state would be so loose and disorganized as to be virtually useless (a replication of the United Nations), or it would have to be so powerful and totalitarian as to have a devastating impact upon personal freedom and human welfare. That is to say, a world state is believed to be totally "unrealistic."

I myself accepted the consensus judgment on this matter until, as an undergraduate student at Fordham University in the early 1960s, I experienced what can only be described as a "vision" of social progress on a global scale. This vision continues to inspire me to this day—albeit I have been made unhappily aware of how extremely difficult it is to communicate this particular vision to others. But despite many disappointments over the years, I continue to harbor the hope that the problem is not so much with the vision itself, as it is with my limited powers of communication, and that eventually the vision will be shared by a significant number of others. The fundamental elements of the original vision of the early 1960s are as follows.

There are three primary obstacles to the formation of a viable and effective world state: (1) a deep-seated ideological conflict between democratic market capitalism and oligarchic planned socialism; (2) the tremendous economic gap between the living standards of the richest and poorest nations of the world; and (3) the tremendous force of nationalism in the modern world. These obstacles are obviously formidable—but they are not impervious.

As to the ideological gap between the communist and noncommunist worlds, this gap could be bridged by a democratic market socialist system. Such a system would incorporate two basic principles from the noncommunist side: the market system and political democracy. It would also incorporate one basic principle from the communist side: socialism, as defined by public ownership of the preponderance of land and capital. Since its introduction into mainstream economic thinking in the 1930s by Oskar Lange, the market socialist concept has undergone considerable development. Of the several possible varieties of market socialism, that one which seems to me the most promising *in a practical sense* is profit-oriented market socialism.

Under this variety, most large-scale business enterprises would be publicly owned, but they would be instructed and motivated to maximize their profits. Thus, the economy would operate almost identically to the market capitalist economic system as it currently operates in the United States, in the nations of Western Europe, and, to an increasing extent, in many other nations of the world. The salient difference would be that the profits of the publicly owned business enterprises, instead of going, as they do under capitalism, mostly to a small minority of wealthy capitalists, would instead be equitably returned to the working population as a social dividend proportion to earned labor income. My own particular variant of profit-oriented market socialism I dubbed "pragmatic market socialism." Throughout my career as an academic economist, I kept up a steady stream of contributions on market socialism in general and pragmatic market socialism in particular, comprising to date three books and approximately 25 journal articles. For the interested reader, a good entry point into this work is my 1997 book: *Economic Justice: The Market Socialist Vision.*

While the case for pragmatic market socialism is indeed extremely sound just based on the adverse internal characteristics of contemporary Western capitalism (specifically, the extravagantly unequal distribution of capital wealth), the decisive aspect of this case in my own mind was the external situation, i.e., the international situation. At the time of the original vision in the 1960s, obviously the ideological confrontation between communism and noncommunism was the most immediate and ominous peril to human destiny. This confrontation was fueling a nuclear arms competition which threatened to engulf the world in a devastating nuclear war. In a practical sense, this situation made the "external" case for pragmatic market socialism (its potential role as a bridge over the ideological gap) far more important than the "internal" case (its potential role as an antidote to extravagantly unequal capital wealth distribution).

As of the early 1990s, of course, the external case for pragmatic market socialism largely disappeared owing to the collapse of the Soviet Union. The successor states to the ex-Soviet Union and its erstwhile satellites thereafter made haste to replicate democratic market capitalism, as practiced in the leading Western nations, within their own societies. It seems inevitable that the People's Republic of China and the other remaining communist nations will eventually follow the Soviet example. Therefore, the ideological war between communism and noncommunism is ostensibly in its final stages, and noncommunism has apparently won the war. Although pragmatic market socialism is no longer required as an ideological bridge between East and West, I do not regret the time and energy I devoted to the development of this concept. Pragmatic market socialism would still be a very desirable reform for the contemporary capitalist economies, and it may eventually be recognized as such.

While the precise *degree* of progress in reducing the ideological obstacle to world peace and cooperation might be debated, it is indisputable that this obstacle was at least *significantly reduced* by the collapse of Soviet communism. Clearly the impediments to world government have been correspondingly reduced. But even if the ideological obstacle were to be totally removed, that would still leave two very formidable obstacles fully intact: the economic gap and the force of nationalism.

With respect to the economic gap, what is needed to bridge this gap is a global economic development effort, along the lines of the post-World War II Marshall Plan, but on a far larger and more ambitious scale. The effort should have an explicit purpose: a high degree of equalization of living standards across all nations of the world—subject to the constraint that living standards in the richest nations continue to rise at a reasonable rate. The critical question, of course, is whether this objective is feasible: whether it would be possible to achieve a high degree of equalization in living standards across the world, within a reasonable length of time, without incurring either a decline of living standards within the richest nations, or a significant reduction in their rate of rise.

Using the tools of my profession of economics, I personally have developed some important evidence that the answer to this key question is indeed in the affirmative. This evidence, described most extensively in my book *Common Progress: The Case for a World Economic Equalization Program* (2000), consists of simulation experiments with a computer model of the world economy. Results from these simulations suggest that a very substantial degree of equalization in world living standards might be achieved within a planning period of only 50 years, at a modest cost in terms of a slightly lower rate of rise in the living standards of the richest nations. The prevailing, consensus attitude of contemporary mainstream economics concerning the prospects for dramatic economic progress in the poor nations of the world within the foreseeable future must be described as wearily pessimistic. According to this prevailing attitude, the results which I have obtained from these computer simulations are simply "too good to be true." The conventional wisdom maintains that putting major resources into a worldwide economic development program would be tantamount to pouring these resources down a rat hole—they would be swallowed up by corrupt bureaucrats, and little or nothing would be accomplished in terms of raising the living standards of the general population in the poor nations.

In my opinion, this widely prevalent viewpoint is in fact little more than a superficial rationalization for a policy of shortsighted selfishness. It is both irrational and immoral to dismiss the possibility of a major global economic development effort simply on the *assumption* that such an effort would be futile. The results which I have adduced in this area argue strongly for at least an experimental implementation of such an effort. If the pessimistic attitude just described is in fact borne out, then, indeed, the effort would have to be terminated. But at least the rich nations could then terminate their resource contributions to the worldwide economic development program with a clear conscience—because it would have been empirically demonstrated that the program was not achieving its objectives.

If a substantial amount of economic equalization *cannot* be achieved within a reasonable period of historical time, then the prospects for a viable, permanent and effective world government are indeed very slight. But just as it is irrational and immoral to simply *assume* that a worldwide economic development program would be unsuccessful, so too it is irrational and immoral to simply *assume* that a world government would be unsuccessful. Just as a worldwide economic development program deserves a fair chance to prove itself, so too does a world government. But it cannot be just *any* world government. It is necessary to think very carefully about what is possible and what is not possible at the present juncture in human history. It is necessary to develop a specific proposal for world government which achieves an acceptable balance between the competing objectives of establishing a useful supernational government entity, and, at the same time, protecting the legitimate interests of the existing nation-states. Regrettably, it seems that the majority of proponents of world government in the past have been inadequately concerned with the very serious problems confronting world government, and inadequately assiduous in trying to find specific institutional proposals that respond adequately to these problems. Many of these proponents seem to imagine a government with strong central powers, along the lines of the contemporary United States of America, immediately established, with all the nations of the world, without exception, voluntarily subjecting themselves to this government. In the judgment of this author, there is simply no feasible way of getting from here to there, at least in the absence of some horrific global catastrophe such as a nuclear World War III.

My own effort to find a solution to the ideological obstacle to world government was the concept of pragmatic market socialism. It appears that this concept is no longer needed for this purpose—and that is all well and good, since the potential contribution of world government to human welfare is far more important than the potential contribution of pragmatic market socialism. Again, my own effort to find a bridge over the economic gap is the worldwide economic development program discussed above. The continuing need for such a program is, to my mind, self-evident. Were such a program implemented, it would, in due course, very likely eliminate the economic obstacle to world government. This would leave the power of nationalism as the third and last major obstacle to world government. I have attempted to cope with this obstacle by means of a carefully considered institutional proposal for world government tentatively designated the Federal Union of Democratic Nations. The basic elements of this proposal are as follows:

The Federal Union of Democratic Nations would be a legitimate, full-fledged state entity with the power to promulgate and enforce laws, the power to levy taxes and engage in public works, and the power to raise and maintain military forces. Its leaders would be directly elected by the citizens and its administrative apparatus would be substantial and in continuous operation. It would have a capital city, regional offices, and the standard symbols of state authority: a flag, an anthem, emblems, and so on.

At the same time, there would be several key restrictions on the power and authority of the supernational federation in order to forestall possible tendencies toward totalitarianism. To begin with, as suggested by its name, the Federal Union would be a federal, rather than a unitary, state. That is, it would supplement—not replace—the national states taking membership in it. These member nations and their respective governments would not merely be formal entities within the supernational federation; they would retain substantial degrees of sovereignty, autonomy, and independence. Key restraints on the supernational state would include the following: (1) member nations would retain the right to raise and maintain military forces; (2) member nations would retain the right to withdraw (secede) from the supernational federation at their own unilateral discretion; and (3) a dual voting principle would be employed in the legislative assembly.

Formally established by a Federal Union Constitution, the Federal Union of Democratic Nations would comprise the standard three branches of government: (1) a legislative arm called the Union Chamber of Representatives; (2) an executive arm guided by a Union Chief Executive; and (3) a judicial arm called the Union High Court. All three would be directly elected by the population: Union Representatives would have terms of five years, the Union Chief Executive a term of ten years, and Union Justices terms of 25 years. Component branches of the executive arm would include the Ministry of the Interior, Ministry of Finance, Ministry of Justice, Ministry of Science, Education, and Culture, Ministry of Planning, Ministry of External Development, Ministry of Security, Ministry of Non-Union Affairs, and World Development Authority.

The specific institutional proposals are developed in light of the various perceived problems and hazards inherent in the concept of a world state. The first and foremost of these is the possibility that a world state would attempt to impose upon member nations uncongenial social systems (e.g., communism—or capitalism). Second to this, but still extremely important, is the possibility that a world state would attempt quick and drastic redistribution of income and wealth from the richer to the poorer member nations. This potential policy is referred to as "Crude Redistribution," and it is sharply contrasted to the preferred policy of "Common Progress" (by which living standards in *all* nations would increase, but the *rate* of increase would be higher in the poorer nations than in the richer nations). The position which I argue is that a supernational federation will only be feasible and viable if the supernational government totally and unequivocally renounces Crude Redistribution in favor of Common Progress. Many specific proposals are designed to allay fears and apprehensions based on the possibility of misguided social activism and/or Crude Redistribution.

The single most fundamental proposal which would militate against the world state becoming an instrument of oppression is the right of secession. This right would be reinforced by the right of member nations to maintain independent military forces. It is proposed that all military forces of the Union, whether maintained by the member nations or by the Union itself, wear the same uniform, have similar weaponry, and be considered formally as components of the overall Union Security Force. But in the event of fundamental and irreconcilable conflict between the Union and a particular member nation, the nation would have both the formal authority and informal means (i.e., its own military) of resuming its independence from the Union.

Secession would be a drastic step and, if widely prevalent, would threaten the viability and existence of the Federal Union. Certain key proposals are designed to forestall the emergence of such serious conflicts between the Union and its member nations that secession would be contemplated. Among the most important is the dual voting system in the Union Chamber of Representatives. According to this system, any proposed measure would have to be passed by a 60 percent majority on two bases: the population basis and the material basis. In the population vote, a Union Representative's voting weight would be equal to the proportion of the population of the entire Union represented by the population of his or her own Union District. In the material vote, that same Union Representative's voting weight would be equal to the proportion of the overall revenue of the entire Union represented by the revenue raised in that Representative's Union District. Thus, the richer nations, as providers of most of the Union's revenues, would retain more power in the legislature than would be the case if voting weight were based exclusively on population represented.

Although I devote much attention to the "negative" issue of impeding undesirable policies and activities by the supernational federation, substantial attention is also devoted to the "positive" aspects of supernational federation. For example, concentration of the space exploration effort within a single political entity encompassing a very large proportion of the human population might well lead to a more vigorous and successful effort. This effort would be the sole concern of the Ministry of External Development. The same is true of the Union's pursuance of a World Economic Development Program under the guidance of the World Development Authority—with the understanding that this program would be conducted along the lines of Common Progress and not Crude Redistribution.

The psychological importance of the Union as a symbol of human unity and solidarity cannot be overemphasized, and this importance dictates, among other things, that the capital city of the Federal Union must be a very impressive and attractive location. In addition to the usual imposing public buildings, the capital city should contain numerous superior tourist attractions: museums, theaters, a botanical garden, a zoo, and perhaps a major amusement park along the lines of Disneyworld. In short, the capital city should be made into one of the great tourist destinations of the world.

There are many other important practical issues. For example, with respect to immigration, it is conceded that although free movement of goods and capital within the Union should be pursued from the outset, the elimination of the present national barriers to immigration will have to await the success of the World Economic Development Program. With respect to a common language, the argument is that there should be only one official language within the Union, and that this language should be English. The hope would be that this would be made acceptable to non-English-speaking nations by the requirement that all schoolchildren in English-speaking nations study some other language to the same extent and intensity that schoolchildren in other nations study English.

There are various other objectives and areas of activity for the supernational federation. For example, certain organizational and regulatory functions pertaining to international transport, commerce and communications, as well as global environmental protection, some of them already well developed at the present time under the auspices of the United Nations or other multinational entities, could be taken over by appropriate ministries of the Federal Union. It should not be excessively difficult to establish a common currency within the Union under the aegis of the Ministry of the Interior. The Ministry of the Interior could also engage in the collection and dissemination of economic and social statistics pertaining to the member nations. Among the projects of the Ministry of Science, Education, and Culture might be the support of a few elite universities, newly founded by the Federal Union at various locations throughout the federation. The Ministry of Planning would have nothing to do with direct economic planning of the sort that was long favored in the Soviet Union and some other communist nations. Rather it would operate as a permanent, large-scale "think tank," which would carefully analyze and evaluate various policy concepts and proposals emanating in embryonic form from legislators and executives in the supernational government. Its reports would then become inputs into practical decision-making by these legislators and executives.

If the Federal Union of Democratic Nations develops properly, nonmember nations will experience increasing incentives to join the Union. To begin with, participation in the Federal Union free trade area would represent very tangible economic benefits. Moreover, the poorer member nations would receive preferential treatment in the World Economic Development Program. Member nations of the Union would also enjoy more security against the threat of foreign invasion by nonmember nations. But aside from these practical matters, there would be the extremely important, albeit intangible, psychological element in Union membership. The history of nation-states and nationalism, among other things, demonstrates the attractiveness to individual human beings of being part of large-scale social undertakings. Human beings are social animals, and they derive a high degree of comfort and encouragement from active participation in society. All other things being equal, they prefer being part of larger organized social groups than smaller organized social groups. Perhaps it is a matter of some fundamental, primitive impulse toward risk-sharing: the larger the group sharing the risk, the less risk to each individual member of the group. Also no doubt there are considerations of power and capability. As a rule, larger organized social groups possess more power and capability than do smaller organized social groups, and to some extent at least, larger group power and capability tend to translate into tangible benefits to the individual members of the group. The expectation of these benefits in the future creates a psychological incentive to participation, even if the current benefits are not in fact particularly obvious or dramatic.

Of course, the incentives of nonmember nations to join the Union will be greater to the extent that the Union's citizenry maintains a relatively high level of unity and harmony. This is not to say that a utopian condition of beatific bliss is either possible or necessarily desirable. It goes without saying that there will inevitably be a great deal of vigorous, even acrimonious, political discussion and controversy within the Federal Union into the foreseeable future. But such discussion and controversy could and should be conducted within a context of deeply shared purpose and mutual respect. Political issues should generally be regarded as temporary problems and difficulties which will eventually be surmounted by the Federal Union—not as permanent liabilities which call into serious question the fundamental value and very existence of the Federal Union. This positive attitude toward political controversy would be facilitated by the development of what might be termed "supernational patriotism."

There is a subtle interplay between "real factors" and "psychological factors." The real factor in this case is the existence of the Federal Union of Democratic Nations, its physical substance in terms of buildings and people, its active participation in the governance of society. The psychological factor is the impact upon human mentality of the Federal Union, of its provision of a higher focus of loyalty and allegiance than the focus presently provided by the national governments. The more successful the Federal Union is in terms of its practical operations, the more rapidly will the psychological attitude of supernational patriotism grow and progress. At the same time, the more developed becomes the spirit of supernational patriotism, the more successful the Federal Union will tend to become in its practical operations and endeavors. The objective is the simultaneous, interactive development of both real and psychological factors in a kind of snowballing process toward a very high level of effectiveness and unity. It cannot be anticipated that progress will be continuous and linear. No doubt there will be setbacks, periods of retrogression and apprehension, disappointments and defeats. But this has, indeed, been the history of humanity throughout all past ages. Despite all the tragic reverses experienced by humanity throughout its long history, the general trend has definitely been onward and upward. Supernational federation offers us a major opportunity to consolidate, continue, and accelerate the onward and upward trend established by human history up to the contemporary age.

What Can World Federalists Do?

Quite frankly, at the present time world federalists constitute such a tiny fraction of the world population as to be a politically negligible factor. In my opinion, this is not merely unfortunate—it is unnecessary. There are certain quite sensible strategic and tactical modifications that might be made that could—conceivably—win enough additional adherents to the cause of world federalism for the movement to begin making significant, perceptible, meaningful headway. There are five central recommendations I want to advance: (1) specify *limited* world government as the goal; (2) focus on the goal; (3) work through the national governments; (4) renounce scare tactics; and (5) respond rationally to skepticism.

Specify Limited *World Government as the Goal*

If the Federal Union of Democratic Nations, as described in the foregoing, were established in the real world tomorrow, it might take 50 years, 100 years, or possibly even longer, to develop into the kind of extremely authoritative and effective—yet benign—world government that world federalists tend to envision. Most world federalists envision what I am calling "unlimited world government," while the proposed Federal Union of Democratic Nations, in its early stages, would most certainly be a "limited world government." Nevertheless, the Federal Union would clearly be a "government" in the strict sense of the term, with democratically elected legislative, executive and judicial branches, a capital city, a permanent administrative apparatus, authority to tax, authority to maintain military forces, and a range of symbolic elements including flag, anthem, insignia and trappings. In my books on world government I have provided what I hope is a happy medium between too much and too little in the way of proposed institutions and procedures. It would be beyond the scope of this relatively brief essay to get into these details. Readers who are interested in the details are referred to my books.

It is impossible to predict exactly how much or how little the Union would be able to accomplish in its first few decades. At a minimum, it would provide a regular forum for continuous meetings and discussions. Some of these meetings and discussions might be productive in terms of resolutions as well as substantive legislation and policies. The main thing in the early stages would be the resolute and energetic prosecution of the global economic development effort. The success or failure of the World Economic Equalization Program, in all probability, will determine the success or failure of the Federal Union of Democratic Nations. The extreme economic differentials among nations that exist today constitute an extremely difficult impediment to achieving international consensus in a variety of problem areas, especially those having to do with population, migration, and the environment. If and when a reasonable level of economic homogeneity among the nations is achieved, they will be able to perceive these problem areas more similarly, and thus will be able to respond to them more effectively.

The long-term goal, of course, is a world in which all or most of the human population has been freed from the fear of suffering and dying in the course of organized violence and warfare. It would be a world in which the military establishments of the nations would be a small fraction of their present dimensions, and in which stocks of weapons of mass destruction, both nuclear and non-nuclear, would had dwindled to vestigial levels or been eliminated altogether. It would be a world in which localized wars such as the Iran-Iraq war of the 1980s would be impossible, because the Federal Union would not permit them to occur. It would be a world in which internal civil wars such as those in Bosnia, Rwanda and the Sudan would also be impossible, also because the Federal Union would not permit them to occur.

But it is unlikely that the present generation of humanity will live long enough to witness the achievement of this particular goal. In its early stages, it would be unwise for the Federal Union to dissipate its resources trying to quell localized conflict situations involving nonmember nations. These situations should probably be allowed to burn themselves out, in the process providing the rest of the world with instructive lessons in the adverse consequences of tyranny and anarchy. (However, as soon as the nations involved in these situations join the Union, they would come under its protection.) No doubt some world federalists would be repelled by this apparently inhumane attitude. But the fact is that the militarily powerful nations of the world are not now, nor will they be for a long time to come, willing to invest substantial human and material resources to quell localized conflict situations in remote corners of the world. This would continue to be the case even if a Federal Union of Democratic Nations were established.

But once the Union had been established, it would foster gradual growth of psychologically integrative forces, and these forces would eventually create conditions under which the Union's citizens would not stand idly by while crimes against humanity were being perpetrated anywhere in the world. The willingness of the Union to suppress these crimes would be a powerful deterrent against their occurrence. It is no use bemoaning the fact that this situation does not yet exist in the world. The important thing now is simply to establish a supernational federation that possesses the *potential* to evolve gradually into the powerful agent of peace and progress which is necessary if humanity is to realize a bright future.

As I asserted at the beginning of this essay, I believe firmly that there does exist a plausible transition path leading from the system of national sovereignty that dominates the world today, to a benign and effective global government of the future. The path to an *extremely* effective global government may require many decades, possibly even centuries, to traverse. But this path is not of merely academic interest to people today. This is because there is another path to a *somewhat* effective, *limited* global government, such as the Federal Union of Democratic Nations, that might be traversed within a few short years. The short path to limited world government in the immediate future is the first stage on the longer path to an unlimited world government of the relatively distant future. It is very doubtful that humanity will ever be willing to make an instantaneous jump to unlimited world government. There is too much of a gap between such a world government and the present system of national sovereignty. There is a much smaller gap between the present system and a limited world government along the lines of the Federal Union of Democratic Nations. This much smaller gap is a gap that the nations of the world might seriously consider jumping over.

As the developer of the proposal for a Federal Union of Democratic Nations, of course I personally would be greatly honored if the world federalist movement, which at the moment is dissipating its energies in many different directions, were to coalesce around this proposal. To my knowledge, no other practical, concrete proposal for limited world government has been developed and defended in such detail as the proposal for a Federal Union of Democratic Nations set forth in my books *World Union on the Horizon* and *Rethinking World Government*. I am not saying that this proposal is correct in every detail, and of course I welcome constructive criticism from anyone who might be interested. But I think it would be healthy for the world federalist movement if its adherents could respond with a degree of uniformity to the inevitable skeptical question: "What exactly do you intend by 'world government'?"

Whatever specific plan for world government is settled upon by the world federalist movement, it must necessarily be a plan for limited world government in which, at a bare minimum, the member nations would retain the right to maintain whatever military establishments they want under their direct control, and the right to depart peacefully from the federation whenever they desire. Without these stipulations, very few nations of the contemporary world will give any consideration whatsoever to joining the supernational federation.

Focus on the Goal

Many world federalists today, perhaps the great majority, have given up on their long-term aspiration toward a genuine global government. They believe it is no longer worthwhile to expend energy and effort trying to achieve this goal. This is a most unfortunate mistake. The fact is that genuine global government within our own lifetimes *is* an achievable goal—albeit this would be a *limited* world government along the lines of the Federal Union of Democratic Nations. Such a world government, in all probability, would not enjoy universal membership upon its initiation. It might well take many decades for universal membership to be achieved. It might *never* be achieved. But even if universal membership is never achieved, this is not necessarily a problem. The nation of Switzerland never bothered to join the United Nations. The United Nations obviously has its weaknesses, shortcomings and limitations. But the non-adherence of Switzerland is not an important reason for them.

Nor would the Federal Union of Democratic Nations, in its early years, be so omnipotent in world affairs that it would easily suppress such tragedies as the ongoing genocide in Darfur, or to make dramatic progress toward protecting and preserving the natural environment. What the Federal Union *would* do is to put into place an institutional structure that would enable a process of evolutionary development to commence that ultimately *would* successfully address these issues. World federalists today will almost certainly not live long enough to witness the culmination of the process, but they may very well live long enough to witness its commencement—*if* they will focus sufficiently on the attainable goal of limited world government. It is said that the best is the enemy of the good. It certainly seems that the world federalist movement, having given up trying to achieve the "best," i.e., an unlimited world government, is at the same time abandoning the opportunities that do exist to achieve, within the relatively near future, the "good," i.e., a limited world government

Symptomatic of what I see as misdirection in the world federalist movement is the recent merger of the World Federalist Association with the Campaign for UN Reform to create Citizens for Global Solutions (CGS). CGS devotes almost all of its limited resources to such minor, short-term issues as the getting the United States government to (1) support the International Criminal Court, (2) put pressure on the Sudan government to end the genocide in Darfur, (3) get out of Iraq—or at least to admit that getting into Iraq was a mistake, (4) so on and so forth. Apparently it is no accident that the organization's name omits any mention of world government or world federalism. The leadership of CGS is apparently of the belief that any such mention would be off-putting to potential supporters and contributors.

I am not saying that the goals of CGS are not worthy goals. What I am saying, however, is that these goals are already supported by a wide swath of the population: basically by almost all those who are slightly left-of-center and who favor a generally peaceful and cooperative approach for the United States in its international relations, as opposed to a truculent and confrontational approach. The vast majority of these people, at the present time, can envision no role whatsoever for world government anytime within the next hundred years or more. They cannot think outside the box of national sovereignty. They believe that the hope of the world lies in the awakening of all the nations of the world to the fact that their long-term interests would be best served by a policy of cooperation and accommodation ("niceness") toward all other nations—but they have not yet themselves awakened to the fact that this awakening would be facilitated and hastened by the immediate establishment of a limited federal world government along the lines of the Federal Union of Democratic Nations. They are certainly correct that the best hope for humanity on this planet lies in nations becoming "nicer" toward one another than they have been in the past. But they are incorrect in thinking that world government cannot be a means toward this end.

The Campaign for UN Reform, as it name suggested, was always first and foremost a UN support organization dedicated primarily to getting the United States to ante up its UN assessments. But the name of the World Federalist Association indicated a primary focus on actual, genuine world government. Not all the membership of the old WFA was happy about the national WFA being absorbed into CGS. The Northern California branch of WFA "revolted" and set up a new organization called Democratic World Federalists (DWF). The new name suggests that the organization has not lost sight of the traditional world federalist goal. But quite a substantial proportion of DWF output in terms of newsletters and e-mails has no discernible connection with world government. A great deal of it seems to consist of vociferous criticism of the present U.S. administration ("Bush-bashing"). Personally, I do not believe that Bush-bashing does any good at all in awakening the citizens of the United States, or of any other country in the world, to the positive contribution that a limited world government would make toward ensuring a benign future for the human race.

There are tens of millions of people in the United States today who are inclined toward Bush-bashing. I count myself among them. I think George W. Bush is one of the most intellectually and attitudinally limited Presidents the United States has ever had. If it had not been for the 9/11 disaster, his standing in the history of the Presidency would have been comparable to that of Franklin Pierce or Millard Fillmore. The Bush administration fell under the influence of naïve neo-cons who over-estimated the benefits of invading Iraq (apparently there never were any WMDs there), and far worse, they disastrously under-estimated both the military and material costs that would have been needed to establish a prosperous, democratic Iraq following the ouster of the Saddam Hussein regime. Instead of that, Iraq is hovering on the brink of all-out civil war that will bring further ruination upon that unhappy nation. Mistakes of this magnitude often lead to regime change, especially if the nation enjoys democratic institutions. Owing to the two-term limit on the U.S. Presidency, George W. Bush will leave office in early 2009. It seems almost inconceivable that the United States will continue its military intervention in Iraq much beyond that year—unless there occurs a veritably miraculous improvement in conditions there. But the ending of the U.S. intervention in Iraq will not bring us any closer toward fundamental transformation of the current national sovereignty system.

I believe that it is a waste of world federalist resources to pursue such goals as ending the U.S. intervention in Iraq. There are millions and millions of people pursuing that particular goal. What distinguishes world federalists from people who simply want the nations of the world, especially the United States, to be "nicer" toward other nations, is that we recognize, as they do not, that the "more niceness" goal could be more successfully pursued if it were supported by a federal world government—albeit a *limited* federal world government. World federalists should focus on spreading awareness of this fundamental reality throughout all sections of society, including the professional intelligentsia, the political leadership, and the general public. Otherwise we will continue to be just a minor, inconsequential, "me too" contributor to contemporary political discourse.

Work through the National Governments

When it first became evident, back in the late 1940s, that the national governments were not going to support the establishment of a genuine world government that would go beyond that ineffectual international debating society known as the United Nations, some world federalists took refuge in the notion of initiating a grass-roots campaign that would soon swell up into a massive political movement that would "force" the national governments to establish world government. Various "people's conventions" were organized, such as the People's World Convention that met in Geneva, Switzerland, in December 1950. The Geneva convention was attended by more than 500 delegates from 47 nations. However, none of the 500 delegates was an authorized representative of any national government. The convention continued for seven days during which the participants argued themselves to a standstill on all significant issues. There was too little consensus regarding the institutional structure of a world government. Aside from that, the vast majority of the world's population by that time believed that the emerging Cold War between East and West rendered any sort of world government thoroughly unrealistic.

But the idea of a "people's movement" to "force" the recalcitrant national governments to form a world government refused to die. The single most impressive effort to implement this strategy during the last half of the twentieth century was probably that of Philip Isely, founder and until recently Secretary-General of the World Constitution and Parliament Association (WCPA), an organization whose historical roots lay in the heady years just following World War II, when best-selling books and world-renowned scientists, statesmen and humanitarians were proclaiming the need for world government. The Association has organized a considerable number of international conferences from the 1960s onwards. One of these conferences, termed the second session of the World Constituent Assembly, held at Innsbruck, Austria, in June 1977, ratified the initial version of the Constitution for the Federation of Earth. The document carries the signatures of approximately 150 individuals from many different nations. An amended version was ratified at the fourth session of the World Constituent Assembly, held at Troia, Portugal, in May 1991, and carries the signatures of well over 200 individuals. Some of the signatories to these versions, such as Linus Pauling of the United States, Tony Benn of the United Kingdom, and Desmond Tutu of South Africa, are well-known figures. However, none of them were operating as authorized representatives of a national government at the time they signed. Readers interested in more detail on the program and activities of the WCPA are referred to two books by Errol E. Harris: *One World or None: A Prescription for Survival* (1993), and *Earth Federation Now! Tomorrow Is Too Late* (2005).

Under the terms of the Constitution, a Provisional World Parliament has met on several occasions during the 1980s and 1990s, and has passed a number of legislative bills. World Legislative Bill Number One (Sept. 11, 1982), for example, carries the title: "To Outlaw Nuclear Weapons and Other Weapons of Mass Destruction." The bill specifies the establishment of a World Disarmament Agency (WDA), but enforcement of the WDA's decisions is to be left to political units (cities, counties, provinces, states, etc.) within nations whose national governments have ratified the bill. To date, no national governments have in fact ratified World Legislative Bill Number One. Indeed, it is probably fair to say that despite prodigious effort by Philip Isely and a handful of colleagues over several decades, only a tiny handful of people throughout the contemporary world are even aware of the existence of the World Constitution and Parliament Association and its various affiliates, and of those few, most would categorize the participants in these organizations as lunatic fringe political enthusiasts.

In my view, the failure of the WCPA to attract sufficient support to realize its objective is not that the name "Federation of Earth" sounds like it came from the pages of a science fiction novel. Rather it is that the WCPA's Federation would be an unlimited world government, as opposed to a limited world government. In this respect it is similar to Borgese's Federal Republic of the World and Clark-Sohn's strengthened United Nations. But in addition to this fundamental flaw, the WCPA's efforts were weakened by its distain for the national governments, by its belief that national government officials would have to be dragged along by the ear, like squalling children, by the good and noble "people" in order for world government to be achieved. The tone of WCPA literature, which continually harps on the dichotomy between "the people" and "governments," would be off-putting to anyone who had worked hard to get himself or herself elected to public office. If any of these people happened to become aware of the existence of the WCPA and read some of its literature, they would probably not be inclined toward sympathetic interest.

Especially in democratic nations such as the United States, the nations of Western Europe, and so on, there is a remarkably large concurrence between the perceptions and preferences of the population as a whole, and the perceptions and preferences of the political leadership. Of course, human nature being what it is, there is a wide spectrum of opinion within the general population on any specific political issue. In order to be elected, aspiring government officials need to appeal to a fairly wide range of people in the middle of any particular spectrum. This clearly encourages a certain amount of vagueness and ambiguity in the candidate's speeches and other statements. Excessive candor might alienate parts of the electorate and lead to the candidate's loss of the election. Some might deem this "dishonesty" on the candidate's part, and to go further to the assertion that the most successful candidates are likely to be those who are the most dishonest. Such assertions, in my view, are dangerously counter-productive. Certainly the need for vagueness and ambiguity to win elections is one downside of democracy, but as Winston Churchill remarked: "Democracy is the worst political system on earth—except for all the others that have been tried." A more positive way to look at "ambiguity" is that the candidates are seeking sufficient "consensus" among the electorate to provide a firm foundation for progressive action by the government.

It would be beyond the scope of this essay to tackle the pros and cons of democracy, and how it might be improved without harm to the basic principle of "sovereignty of the majority." But it is my firm belief that notwithstanding all its faults, democracy as it is practiced in the United States and kindred nations has the effect of putting into national government offices a fairly representative cross-section of the general population. I would judge that in order to be elected to a high national government office, a person would have to be at least somewhat above average in terms of intelligence and articulateness, but that his or her beliefs and opinions must be quite representative of those not too far to the right or the left of the "overall spectrum" of political opinion, as opposed to the opinion spectrum on any specific issue. The implication of this, as far as world federalists are concerned, is that it will not be any more or less difficult to persuade a national government official to embrace world federalism, than it would be to persuade any given member of the general public to do this.

The corollary of this point is that in order to achieve world government, it will be necessary to work through the national governments. A sufficient majority of the general population must be persuaded of the benefits of world government to induce a democratically elected national government to be so persuaded. While the enlightenment campaign is being conducted among the general public, it should simultaneously be conducted among the political leadership. It is not a matter of first persuading the general public, following which the general public will go to the political leadership and demand that progress be made toward world government. The elected leadership is drawn from the general public, and remains part of the general public even after being elected. I would therefore urge world federalists to discontinue any and all rhetoric that explicitly or implicitly denigrates the intelligence, character, and/or motivations of national government officials.

If a Federal Union of Democratic Nations, or some similar form of world government, is established in the real world within our lifetimes, it will be through the same general procedures and processes by which the United Nations was established in 1945. The national governments of prospective member nations of the federation will appoint authorized representatives to an international conference. Following the preparation of a constitution by the conference, each of the national governments will separately approve the constitution and formally join the federation. (Of course, some may decline to do so.) It is necessary that the process of establishing a world government "go through channels," so to speak, and in this case the "channels" refer to the national governments. The idea of making some kind of "end run" around these channels is simply illusory and counter-productive.

Renounce Scare Tactics

Most world federalist literature in the past, and continuing on into the present day, consists of elaborate recitations of the problems and the disasters of the world, and the dire perils confronting humanity in its efforts to survive and thrive on planet Earth. I absolutely agree that if humanity continues with "business as usual" for any prolonged period into the future, the tenure of the human species on this planet might be, in geological terms, exceedingly brief. No doubt we are laying a firm foundation for our own destruction, either by nuclear holocaust, catastrophic environmental breakdown, or some combination of the two. Nevertheless, I don't see that harping on this fact will be helpful to the cause of world government. Simply from the past history of the world federalist movement, it should be apparent that scare tactics will not work. Even at the height of the Cold War, when instantaneous nuclear disaster was a heartbeat away, this awful reality did not induce any significant percentage of the world population to give serious consideration to world government as a means of reducing the threat. Instead most people comforted themselves with the delusion that nuclear world war was virtually impossible because it would be so disastrous. With the demise of the Cold War, most of the world's population has entirely dismissed the nuclear threat—despite the fact that the United States, the Russian Federation, and several other nations, retain tens of thousands of nuclear warheads.

As for environmental catastrophe, that is too far off in the future to be of concern to most people. In response to dire jeremiads issued by a handful of environmental enthusiasts and preservationists, the majority might approve a little bit more in the way of environmental regulations, taxes on toxic emissions, and suchlike. But if the majority would not consider world government to allay the threat of nuclear holocaust in the 1960s through the 1980s, they are not going to consider world government as a means of maintaining a benign environment in the early decades of the 21st century. For one thing, environmental jeremiads have less effect now than in the past because a number of environmental doomsday dates have come and gone without evident disaster occurring. For example, many of the simulations done for the 1972 Club of Rome report on "The Limits of Growth" indicated that by the year 2000 an earthly hell would have befallen humanity. That year has come and gone, but those who would describe the current situation, in terms of the physical environment, as an "earthly hell" are dismissed by most people (and rightly so in my opinion) as equivalent to wild-eyed fanatics dressed in burlap wandering along busy sidewalks and carrying signs reading "The End Is Near."

Simply pointing to world problems will not be effective. Most people are already well aware of these problems, but they do not believe that world government is a viable and attractive solution to these problems. In other words, they believe that world government would be a "cure worse than the disease." The task confronting world federalists is to try to make people see that this belief is invalid—that a properly designed, limited world government would indeed provide a mechanism for coping more effectively with world problems, and at the same time it would be reasonably immune from the possibility that it would degenerate into a horrific global tyranny. The argument should be changed from "World government—or else!" to "World government will improve humanity's odds of success in confronting an uncertain future." The latter argument may not be as dramatic as the former, but it is more believable. And believability, in the end, determines an argument's persuasiveness. In formulating the argument, moreover, it must be taken into account that most people today are not currently in a state of dire anxiety about the condition of the world as a whole and humanity as a whole.

The fact is that at the present moment humanity is doing fairly well, thank you. Not that difficulties do not exist, but relative to the abundant past difficulties which fill up the history books, they are not that bad. At the moment, no world war is going on. The genocide in Darfur pales compared to the genocide conducted in Western Europe by the Nazi regime during the war years. The civil wars of the present day are bad, but not as bad as the U.S. Civil War of 1861-1865. There are no plagues at the moment comparable to the Black Death that wiped out half the population of Europe in the 1350s. There are no gigantic wars of conquest at the moment such as those mounted in past centuries by Romans, Huns, Mongols and Muslims. Living standards are rising throughout the world, albeit they are rising much faster in the rich countries than in the poor countries, with the consequence that the economic gap between rich and poor countries is getting steadily wider. In addition to the fact that for most people in the world today, life is as prosperous and secure as it has ever been in the past, one must take into account the fact that appeals to fear of premature death are often ineffective simply because death eventually comes to all human beings no matter what. People will not undertake what they consider to be measures that will seriously endanger their accustomed lifestyles, simply to slightly increase their expected lifespan. They will not want to enter a world federation, if they believe that the main benefit would simply be a slight improvement in their expected lifespan, if they also believe that such a federation would entail a serious risk of economic and/or political tyranny.

What I consider to be a helpful metaphor is as follows. Without an effective world government, humanity is comparable to a group of people drifting down a broad, quiet, unknown river in a boat that is not equipped with either an engine or a rudder. Around the next bend in that river might be raging rapids or a huge waterfall. If so, a boat without an engine or a rudder will not survive, nor will its occupants. As for the notion that we can equip the boat with an engine and a rudder once the rapids or the waterfall come into sight, that assumes that there will enough time to do so—quite possibly an invalid assumption.

Of course, maybe there are no rapids or waterfalls ahead on the river, so that if we continue drifting down it indefinitely we will eventually emerge into a deep, blue, quiet sea. In this case, we would never need the engine and the rudder, and installing them would have been a waste of time and energy. Or, perhaps, the engine and rudder that we might install will be too weak to do any good should we be unlucky enough to encounter rapids and/or a waterfall. Once again, the installation of the engine and the rudder would have been a waste of time and energy. But even if either of these two cases happened to be true, these possibilities are not good arguments against installing an engine and a rudder—unless it is assumed that the "wastage of time and energy" to install an engine and a rudder would be extreme, or that it would somehow be too risky to install them. Such assumptions would be hard to justify on a reasonable basis.

Formation of a world government would be like installing an engine and a rudder on a boat that is drifting down a broad, quiet river. There is no obvious and immediate need for a world government, just as there is no obvious and immediate need for an engine and a rudder on that boat. But just as things might suddenly go wrong for the boat, so too things might suddenly go wrong for humanity. One possibility, made more obvious by the events of September 11, 2001, is that of terrorist action. The most portentous terrorist action of the twentieth century has to be the assassination, on June 28, 1914, of the Archduke Francis Ferdinand, heir to the throne of the Austro-Hungarian empire, and his wife, by a 17-year old Serbian nationalist, one Gavrilo Princip. At first, few expected that the agitated negotiations that followed this outrage would lead to war. Nevertheless, as history duly recorded, they did lead to World War I. Since World War II was a direct outgrowth of World War I, it also must be attributed to Gavrilo Princip. This is what can happen, in a world of sovereign nation-states, as a consequence of one single criminal act by one single fanatic. In the aftermath of the Archduke's assassination, there was no time for the people of the world to reflect on the possibility that with a world government in existence, possibly these crises would not happen, and therefore possibly we should establish a world government. There was no time for that—just as there would be no time for the occupants of the above-mentioned book to install an engine and a rudder once a huge waterfall had come into view.

Respond Rationally to Skepticism.

Proponents of major social policy innovations in the past have tended to be extremely confident that the benefits of these innovations would far outweigh the costs. Or if they had any doubts on this score, they kept these doubts to themselves. They argued the virtues of their proposals with an enthusiasm bordering on fanaticism, and dismissed critics and opponents as either mental incompetents or hypocrites in the pay of "vested interests." If they were heeded and their proposals implemented, then, normally, unanticipated adverse consequences would quickly surface, so that the net benefits of the transition would be less than expected, sometimes far less than expected.

In some cases, the proposed cure was indubitably far worse than the disease. One thinks immediately of Karl Marx, who proclaimed the socialist millennium with all the faith and zeal that one normally associates with religious fanatics. Within a few decades of Marx's death, what should have been the workers' paradise of the Soviet Union was transformed into a totalitarian nightmare presided over by Joseph Stalin, who may not have been a monster to begin with, but who had certainly evolved into one by the time of his death. No doubt Stalin, who died comfortably enough of old age in 1953 after slaughtering millions of his own countrymen, never experienced any significant self-doubt. No doubt he convinced himself that his own personal survival and continued undisputed leadership of the Soviet Union was hastening the glorious socialist millennium promised by Karl Marx. From the ideas and idealism of Karl Marx to the concentration camps and firing squads of Joseph Stalin—such can be the disastrous outcome of sympathetic concern for all humanity and innovative social thinking.

As a result of the real-world disaster initiated by the social theories and prescriptions of Karl Marx, as well as a host of similar experiences throughout human history, a large proportion of both the intelligentsia and the general human population have today lapsed into unimaginative conservatism and thoughtless opposition to almost any significant social transformation, let alone world government. This is most unfortunate, since continued social innovation and progress is probably no less important to the further development of human civilization, and to the further enhancement of individual human existence, than continued scientific innovation and progress. However, in light of past history, it is incumbent upon proposers of social innovations to think very carefully about such innovations, to be quite detailed and specific in their formulation, to be quite thorough and balanced in considering possible flaws and problems, and, above all, to be properly circumspect and restrained in presenting the case for these innovations.

Therefore, I need to state here and now, without qualification or equivocation, that as a matter of fact, I personally am *not* completely certain that the effect of a potential future World Economic Equalization Program, or of a potential future Federal Union of Democratic Nations, would be favorable. It is extremely important, in my view, that if either one or both of these initiatives is actually undertaken in the real world, it would be on a tentative, provisional and experimental basis. It would be useless to deny that a non-negligible possibility exists that the World Economic Equalization Program would be a complete failure, that there would be little acceleration in the growth rates of the poor nations and/or a serious decline in the economic status of the rich nations. If that happens (after a reasonable trial period of at least 10 to 15 years), then the program should be cut back drastically or terminated altogether.

It would be equally useless to deny that a non-negligible possibility exists that the Federal Union of Democratic Nations might be a complete failure, for a variety of reasons, including continued pursuit of a World Economic Equalization Program which is clearly failing to achieve its mission. If that happens (again after a reasonable trial period), nations should withdraw from the Federal Union, until finally, having been reduced to an impotent rump state, the Federal Union voluntarily terminates its own existence. Such a dissolution would be sad and unfortunate, and an ill omen for the future of humanity. But peaceful dissolution would obviously be preferable to violent dissolution.

The formation of a limited world government along the lines of the proposed Federal Union of Democratic Nations should be looked upon as no more and no less than *a scientific experiment*. Such an experiment is the one and only way we have for achieving truly reliable, convincing and compelling evidence on the potential performance of world government. Whether a world government would be a success or a failure simply cannot be determined, to any reasonably satisfactory level of certitude, on the basis of theoretical speculations and hypothetical musings based on the past history of human civilization. The current situation is simply too novel, too unprecedented, and too unparalleled for past history to provide more than circumstantial and inconclusive indications. The fact is that the only means by which we may ascertain whether a world state would make a positive contribution to the future development of human civilization is to set up a world state and then observe the outcome. What is needed is not more words but rather experimental *action*.

It may be found, after an innovation is adopted, that its overall effect is unfavorable. In that case, the innovation could and should be repealed, revoked, discontinued. An interesting case of this sort in United States history was the imposition of a national ban on the production, transportation and sale of alcoholic beverages from 1920 through 1933. Section 1 of the proposed 18th Amendment to the United States Constitution, submitted by Congress to the states in 1917, stated: "After one year from the ratification of this article the manufacture, sale, or transportation of intoxicating liquors within, the importation thereof into, or the exportation thereof from the United States and all territory subject to the jurisdiction thereof for beverage purposes is hereby prohibited." The Amendment was ratified by the requisite number of states by early 1919. Enforcement legislation entitled the National Prohibition Act (popularly known as the "Volstead Act," after Representative Andrew J. Volstead of Minnesota) was passed by Congress on Oct. 28, 1919, over the veto of President Woodrow Wilson. The ban went into effect on January 29, 1920.

Within a short period of time, the costs of "legislating morality" became obvious. Millions of otherwise law-abiding citizens ignored the ban, resulting in a thriving illegal black market supplied by organized crime. Violence erupted in the streets as rival gangs fought to gain control over the illicit but lucrative trade. Corruption spread widely through the enforcement agencies as some of the abundant revenues were diverted to bribes to gain the complicity of the police. The quality of illegal alcohol degenerated, leading to much death and disability among the consuming public. Anyone who wonders what the "war on alcohol" was like during the 1920s has only to look at the "war on drugs" being waged today.

After a decade of experience suggesting that in this case the cure was worse than the disease, the pendulum of public opinion swung against prohibition. By the latter 1920s, anti-prohibition forces were well-organized in the Association Against the Prohibition Amendment (AAPA). The Democratic candidate for President in 1928, Alfred E. Smith, was strongly in favor of repeal of prohibition. Although defeated in the election, Smith's advocacy of repeal legitimized the repeal movement. The onslaught of the Great Depression in 1930 may have put the final nail in prohibition's coffin. To the other arguments against prohibition was now added the assertion that a legal liquor industry would add thousands of new, legal jobs paying taxable income. Another argument at that time might have been that legalized alcohol would help people to cope peaceably with the new economic adversity: clearly, drunkenness might be preferable to the insurrection being preached by the newly socialized Soviet Union. In any event, by the early 1930s the repeal movement was in full swing. The 21st Amendment to the U.S. Constitution, whose principal purpose was simply the repeal of the 18th Amendment, was ratified before the end of 1933. And that marked the end of what Herbert Hoover, defeated in the election of November 1932 for U.S. President by Franklin D. Roosevelt, referred to as "the noble experiment."

Whether the episode had been noble or ignoble, Hoover's use of the term "experiment" is informative. Throughout the many decades prior to the 1920s during which the controversy had raged, advocates and opponents of prohibition had speculated endlessly about the probable effects of a national ban on alcoholic drink. Advocates forecast the moral regeneration of a nation no longer plagued by intoxication and alcoholism. Opponents forecast a narrow and joyless existence presided over by puritanical religious zealots. But no one *really* knew what would happen. When the pro-prohibition forces finally got the upper hand and pushed through the national ban, the anti-prohibition forces howled their lamentations. As it turned out, they should have shouted their hosannas. Within ten years, the compelling evidence provided by actual experience with prohibition swung the overwhelming weight of public opinion over to the anti-prohibition side of the controversy. The political strength of prohibitionist sentiment was soon rendered negligible, and the national ban on alcoholic beverages was quickly lifted. Ten years of actual experience with prohibition were worth more than ten decades of speculative controversy.

Opponents of world government today should keep this historical incident well in mind. Assuming they are correct, then very shortly after the formation of a world government, its disadvantages and liabilities will begin to manifest themselves in a very clear and obvious manner. Perhaps, despite all the admonitions and warnings against attempting to make the world state into an instrument for the radical redistribution of current income, the high officials of the world state will set themselves resolutely toward this course of action. Against opposition to this policy, they will threaten to unleash the military and police forces of the world state. Clear evidence would then exist that the apprehensions and anticipations of world government skeptics are fully on-target. If this were to happen, then the world state would dissolve very quickly and very completely. Just as prohibition was abandoned as soon as its disadvantages could no longer be reasonably denied, so too the world state would be abandoned. It would be a very long time—if ever—before humanity would ever again consider experimenting with world government.

Of course, I myself do not believe that there is any significant possibility that were a world government to be established, its high leadership would be so foolish and misguided as to pursue policies which would inevitably be strongly opposed by substantial national populations. Into this category would certainly fall the policy of radical redistribution of current income. I have cited the example of prohibition of alcohol in the United States from 1920 through 1933 only to suggest that the formation of a world government need not be a final, definitive and irrevocable step. If a potential future world government were to be as unsuccessful in practice as was the policy of prohibition of alcohol in the United States during the 1920s, then that world government would quickly follow the same path as that followed by prohibition—into rapid and complete oblivion. But at the same time, most students of social policy recognize in the experience of prohibition in the United States during the 1920s an atypical case.

The rule is that innovative social policies—policies which are finally adopted after decades of vociferous controversy and bitter resistance—are successful rather than unsuccessful. The various vicissitudes and disasters confidently predicted by conservative opponents turn out to be groundless fantasies. Society carries on much as before, and after a while even most of the conservatives become fully reconciled to the changes, and recognize them to be beneficial not only to the larger society, but to themselves as well. Of all of the amendments to the United States Constitution, for example, only the 18th was later repealed because its effects were obviously perverse. The 13th Amendment, abolishing slavery, has not as yet had to be repealed. Nor has the 19th, which granted the right to vote to women. If a world government is established in the real world, I am very confident that it will very quickly be acknowledged as a positive development by all but a small handful of extremely inflexible and reactionary mentalities.

The key point is, however, that my own personal confidence on this score is *not* a vital component of the case to be made for world government. What *is* a vital component of this case is that it would not be impossible, nor even especially difficult, to dissolve a world government that was not developing in a positive way.

No one likes to admit the possibility of being in error. Thus many world federalists will tend to resist my advice that in discussing world government with "non-believers," they exhibit sufficient modesty to admit openly the possibility of being in error. Given the overwhelming consensus at the present time against world government, however, any world federalist who evinces excessive confidence in the rectitude of the case for world government is likely to be viewed as a deluded crackpot whose views may be safely dismissed without consideration. According to experts on conflict resolution, a voluntary concession by one side of a dispute will often lead to a voluntary concession by the other side, which might lead to a breakup of the logjam preventing reasonable compromise by the two parties. If a world federalist admits that he or she might be in error, possibly the non-world federalist will also admit this possibility. The basis might be laid for a serious examination of the issue that might change the mind of the non-world federalist.

Conclusion

Only the most self-deluded world federalist can believe that there exists in the world today perceptible political trends toward the formation of a genuine world government. In my opinion, however, there does indeed exist a non-negligible possibility that the movement might become politically effective within a short time. The absolutely essential precondition for this to happen is for the movement to shift from its present vision of an unlimited world government to a vision of a limited world government along the lines of my proposal for a Federal Union of Democratic Nations, in which the member nations would retain rights of armament and free departure. Only such a limited world government will be given any consideration whatsoever by the nations of the world within the foreseeable future. But if a large proportion of the nations of the world were to unite to form such a federation, a much firmer foundation will have been established toward an extremely authoritative and effective—yet benign—world government of the more distant future.

No, there does *not* exist a plausible transition path leading directly from the national sovereignty system we know today to unlimited world government—or at least a path that can be traversed within the next few decades. But there *does* exist a plausible transition path leading from today's national sovereignty system to a *limited* world government along the lines of the Federal Union of Democratic Nations—a path that might be traversed within just a few short years, let alone decades. It has been my life's dream to see this path discovered and taken. I appeal to the handful of my fellow world federalists to help today's numerous unenlightened people to discover that path. Then all our dreams might be realized. Or at least *begin* to be realized.

References

Borgese, Giuseppe. *Foundations of the World Republic.* Chicago: University of Chicago Press, 1953.

Clark, Grenville, and Louis B. Sohn. *World Peace through World Law: Two Alternative Plans*, 3rd enlarged edition. Cambridge, MA: Harvard University Press, 1966.

Commission on Global Governance (Ingvar Carlsson and Shridath Ramphal, co-chairmen). *Our Global Neighborhood: The Report of the Commission on Global Governance.* New York: Oxford University Press, 1995.

Harris, Errol E. *One World or None: A Prescription for Survival.* Atlantic Highlands, NJ: Humanities Press, 1993.

Harris, Errol E. *Earth Federation Now! Tomorrow Is Too Late.* Radford, VA: Institute for Economic Democracy, 2005.

Isely, Philip. "A Critique of 'Our Global Neighborhood,'" in Errol E. Harris and James A. Yunker, eds., *Toward Genuine Global Governance: Critical Reactions to "Our Global Neighborhood"* (Westport, CT: Praeger, 1999).

Yunker, James A. *World Union on the Horizon: The Case for Supernational Federation.* Lanham, MD: University Press of America, 1993.

Yunker, James A. *Common Progress: The Case for a World Economic Equalization Program.* Westport, Conn.: Praeger, 2000.

Yunker, James A. "Could a Global Marshall Plan Be Successful? Evidence from WEEP Model Simulations," *World Development* 32(7): 1109-1137, July 2004.

Yunker, James A. *Rethinking World Government: A New Approach.* Lanham, MD: University Press of America, 2005.

Yunker, James A. *Political Globalization: A New Vision of Federal World Government.* Lanham, MD: University Press of America, 2007.

5

Should the United States Champion World Government?

In response to the vicissitudes of the twentieth century, which included two devastating world wars during the first half of the century, followed by the threat of an even more devastating nuclear World War III during most of the second half of the century, the possibility of world government attracted an unprecedented amount of interest. Moreover, dramatic technological advances in transportation and communications during the twentieth century greatly reduced the coordination difficulties that bedeviled large-scale political organizations in earlier times. Despite this, a world government has not yet been established, owing to persistent apprehensions that it might pave the way toward some fearful combination of global tyranny, bureaucratic suffocation, and cultural homogenization. Apart from a minuscule minority of world federalist true believers, the overwhelming majority of the global population, of all nationalities and walks of life, is at the present time strongly opposed to world government.

Nevertheless, there remains an inherent attractiveness about the idea of a universal political organization, open to all nations of the world, that would uphold the interests of the entire global human population. Among other things, this political organization would effectively eliminate the age-old curse of warfare from human affairs. Such is the inherent attractiveness of the basic idea of world government that the twentieth century witnessed the creation of two novel international organizations, the League of Nations and the United Nations, that might at some future time be perceived as forerunners of the authoritative and effective—yet benign—global government that eventually came into being.

The United States of America played an instrumental role in the foundation of both the League of Nations and the United Nations. Although the plan for a League of Nations originated in Europe, it was the determined advocacy of U.S. President Woodrow Wilson that ensured that the League would be incorporated into the Treaty of Versailles that concluded World War I.[1] However, Wilson was unable to overcome the resurgence of isolationism consequent upon the brief but costly U.S. participation in the war, and the United States did not join the League. This abstention may have been a factor that emboldened Nazi Germany to embark upon a course of "national regeneration" that soon brought about a resumption of conflict. In historical perspective, the two decades between the end of World War I in November 1918 and the beginning of World War II in September 1939 are seen as merely an uneasy truce separating the two "German wars" of the first half of the twentieth century.

Remaining tendencies in the United States toward isolationism were virtually eliminated during the course of American involvement in World War II from December 1941 through August 1945. U.S. President Franklin D. Roosevelt was the prime mover in the genesis of the United Nations, intended as an improved and strengthened League of Nations.[2] If left to their own devices, neither Winston Churchill of the U.K. nor Joseph Stalin of the U.S.S.R. would have been particularly interested in the U.N. Although institutionally very similar to the League of Nations it replaced, the United Nations was in principle much stronger than its predecessor, mainly because the two world superpowers at the end of the war, the United States and the Soviet Union, were both founding members. Unfortunately for the cause of world peace and progress, these same two superpowers were profoundly divided on ideological issues. The development and spread of nuclear weapons at this same time further complicated the extremely hazardous brew of postwar international relations.

To the handful of world federalists still remaining as of the early 1990s, the decline of Cold War tensions in the wake of the collapse and dissolution of the U.S.S.R. presented humanity with another shining opportunity. Just as the end of World War I saw the establishment of the League of Nations, and the end of World War II saw the establishment of the United Nations, could not the end of the Cold War witness the establishment of a genuine world government of which the League and the U.N. were imperfect harbingers? Two decades later, it is now apparent that this opportunity—if opportunity it was—was not exploited. But an opportunity might still be there, and it might still be exploited. Throughout the perilous Cold War decades, international relations experts and the general public alike were in agreement that the abyss separating communist and non-communist ideology, in and of itself, presented an insurmountable obstacle to federal world government. But in the post-Cold War era, the ideological impediment to world government, if not entirely dead, is clearly moribund. As a consequence, the various hazards inherent in world government are diminished, and the overall case for world government is enhanced.

Should the United States, therefore, champion world government? Should some current or future U.S. president follow in the footsteps of Woodrow Wilson and Franklin D. Roosevelt and push for a new and higher form of international organization than ever before witnessed in the entire history of humanity? The answer to this question depends on the nature of the envisioned world government. If the nature of the proposed world government is left vague or completely undefined, it is not possible to address the question sensibly. The plain, simple fact is that not all world government blueprints are equal. Some are more likely to be successful than others. Thus, we turn now to the critical issue of proper design. Does there exist a plan for federal world government that is sufficiently practicable and promising to be worth implementing? Or at least to be worth *considering* implementing?

The Omnipotent World State

As a shock reaction to the advent of nuclear weapons, the awesome destructive power of which was clearly manifested by the atomic bombings of the unfortunate Japanese cities of Hiroshima and Nagasaki in the closing days of World War II, there occurred in the immediate postwar period a dramatic spike of public interest in world government.[3] The tone was set by such bestsellers as *The Anatomy of Peace* by Emery Reves, *One World or None* by a consortium of authors including Niels Bohr, Leo Szilard, Albert Einstein and J. Robert Oppenheimer, and *The Commonwealth of Man* by Frederick L. Schuman.[4] According to the world federalist message of the time, only the immediate establishment of an absolutely universal and authoritative world government would preserve global human civilization from destruction via nuclear holocaust.

Although many well-known and highly influential individuals signed on, in the end the world government movement never attracted a critical mass of adherents sufficient to make a genuine world government possible in the real world. The consensus opinion was challenged but not overturned: that opinion being that the United Nations, although little more than an international debating society, was the best that could be achieved in light of the emerging global confrontation between the communist and non-communist blocs of nations. The world government boom in the immediate aftermath of World War II turned out to be highly ephemeral. By the outbreak of the Korean War in the summer of 1950, all but a tiny minority of world federalist true believers accepted that the window of opportunity for full-scale world government was now closed.

Although vague notions of a universal political organization encompassing the entire world can be traced back to ancient times, it was not until the modern era, from approximately 1500 A.D. on, that sufficient knowledge was accumulated of the physical geography of the planet Earth and the distribution of humanity over its surface, that these notions began to take on a minimum degree of plausibility.[5] Prior to the twentieth century, however, most plans for universal political organizations, such as the Council of Ambassadors of Émeric Crucé and the Congress of States of Immanuel Kant, envisioned a confederation whose sole purpose would be peacekeeping through collective security.[6] It was not until the twentieth century that the current notion came into full fruition that a world state would be a full-purpose government entity with objectives far beyond mere peacekeeping. But in light of the nuclear threat that emerged in the immediate post-World War II period, greater emphasis than ever before was placed on the world government possessing sufficient military power to suppress all possible challenges to its authority.

A considerable number of specific world government schemes were proposed in the postwar period, all of them strongly influenced by the Declaration issued by the first World Congress of the World Movement for World Federal Government (WMWFG) on August 23, 1947, at Montreux, Switzerland. Most of these schemes were and remain obscure, but two schemes in particular achieved somewhat greater public familiarity, largely because they were presented in books published by prestigious university presses. Giuseppe Borgese's *Foundations of the World Republic*, which proposed a "Federal Republic of the World," was published by the University of Chicago Press in 1953, while all three editions of Grenville Clark and Louis Sohn's *World Peace through World Law* (1958, 1960, 1966), which proposed a "strengthened" United Nations, were published by Harvard University Press.

According to the provisions of the Montreux Declaration, membership in the world federation is to be universal, and disarmament of all member nations would be "to the level of their internal policing requirements." All heavy weaponry, including nuclear weapons, would be monopolized by the world government. No member nation would be allowed independent control of large-scale military units: armies, navies, or air forces. In the latter 1940s, it was still well and vividly remembered that the first step on the path leading to World War II was the rearmament campaign undertaken by Nazi Germany after withdrawing from the League of Nations. Clearly therefore, the Montreux Declaration envisions a very powerful and centralized state entity, that would stand in relationship to its member nations much as the national government of the

United States stands in relationship to the component states. This concept of world government may be conveniently and descriptively designated the "omnipotent world state." The omnipotent world state is, at one and the same time, the ideal of the tiny minority of orthodox world federalists, and the bête noire of the overwhelming majority of world government opponents.

To the world federalist minority, the omnipotent world state is the only means by which global human civilization will permanently preserve itself against destruction through nuclear holocaust and/or environmental breakdown. To the majority of world government skeptics, the omnipotent world state, as a proposed solution to the problems of the world, would be "a cure worse than the disease." Aside from a host of political and cultural issues, there is a bedrock economic impediment to world government. Throughout the twentieth century, what can only be described as an "abyss" gradually opened up between economic living standards in the wealthiest nations and those in the poorest nations. Moreover, a large majority of the human population lives in nations that, by the standards of the leading First World nations, are extremely poor.

When confronted with the notion of a very powerful, democratically controlled world government, people in the wealthy nations are apprehensive that such a government might initiate a global welfare state by which they themselves would be heavily taxed to support entitlements that would mostly benefit people in the poor nations. Meanwhile, people in the poor nations are also leery of world government on economic grounds, fearing that such a government might implement international trade and investment laws that would recreate the exploitative economic relations between rich and poor nations of the colonial era. Whether citizens of rich nations or poor nations, most people are skeptical of world government on grounds—among other things—that it might become a malignant instrumentality through which they would be economically disadvantaged or even despoiled.

Efforts by individual nations to escape this potential economic bondage might result in civil war, and even if that did not happen, a global police state might become necessary to maintain compliance. During the perilous Cold War era, the noted international relations authority Kenneth Waltz dismissed the possibility of world government with the following proclamation: "And were world government attempted, we might find ourselves dying in the attempt, or uniting and living a life worse than death."[7] Waltz had in mind a possible effort by the communist nations to subvert the world government and mold it into a tool of communist expansionism. (Communist ideologues of the same era also dismissed world government on grounds that it might be subverted by the capitalist nations and molded into a tool of socioeconomic reaction.) But whether the envisioned oppressive conditions come about through repugnant social systems, or an excessively egalitarian global welfare state, or a return to colonial exploitation, in each case world government is perceived as the avenue toward these dysfunctional conditions.

Clearly, there exists a non-negligible possibility that an effort to establish the omnipotent world state in the contemporary world could result in a very bleak outcome. But there is virtually no possibility that such a world government could be established in the real world, unless possibly in the aftermath of a nuclear World War III. Even during the most perilous Cold War years, when the possibility of instantaneous nuclear disaster was far greater than it is now, there was no possibility of this happening. During that time people heavily discounted the possibility of nuclear war on the basis of MAD reasoning (mutual assured destruction): surely no national leader would be "stupid enough" to start a nuclear war. Although possibly a case of wishful thinking (what about "miscalculated brinkmanship"?), MAD reasoning provided effective consolation against an otherwise terrifying possibility, and enabled most people to carry on with their lives without an undue amount of psychological stress. In any case, the risk of nuclear war in the near future is now a small fraction of what it was during the worst of the Cold War, and thus any argument based on this risk for world government in the form of the omnipotent world state is even less convincing than it was then.

Nevertheless, it is an error—potentially a dire error—to reject the *general* concept of world government on the basis of the perceived defects of the omnipotent world state. The omnipotent world state is not the only form in which world government might be realized. If we imagine a spectrum of possibilities, in terms of authority and effectiveness, between the United Nations at one end and the omnipotent world state at the other end, there is a wide range of intermediate possibilities in between. The United Nations, although (for most people) "better than nothing" and certainly evidence of the good intentions of a substantial proportion of the human race, nevertheless must be realistically described as possessing little authority and low effectiveness. At the other end of the spectrum, the omnipotent world state would be highly authoritative and effective—the downside of this being that it might all too easily degenerate into global tyranny.

According to the happy medium principle, the optimum point is usually found somewhere between the extreme end points of the spectrum of possibilities. This principle suggests that there might exist some novel form of international organization—of such nature that it that may be sensibly characterized as a "world government"—somewhere between the United Nations and the omnipotent world state. The fact that humanity is not yet ready for a *highly* effective and authoritative world government does not necessarily mean that it is not ready for a *somewhat* effective and authoritative world government.

The horrific events of September 11, 2001, came as a shock to the gradual trend toward increasing complacency initiated by the sudden decline of Cold War anxieties in the early 1990s. One possible manifestation of this shock may have been a certain resurgence of interest in world government among international relations (IR) professionals. In 2003, Alexander Wendt, a well-known IR professor at Ohio State University, and a leading figure in the constructivist school of thought, published an article under the provocative title "Why a World State Is Inevitable."[8] Since its publication this article has attracted considerable interest, as evidenced by its being cited in dozens of contributions to the IR literature. This is not to say that this attention has been uniformly laudatory—far from it. None of the many authors who have commented on Wendt's article have explicitly endorsed the "inevitability proposition."

Wendt's teleological argument is that world government is the logical—and thus inevitable—culmination of a long-term process of political consolidation that has led from the tens of thousands of independent tribal units of prehistory down to the 200-odd nation-states of today. There are some obvious problems with the argument. First, long before the consolidation trend reaches its future culmination in a world state, a devastating nuclear world war might intervene, a war of such overwhelming destructiveness that it might initiate a reverse trend toward the Stone Age level of civilization, or even to the extinction of the human race. Second, in the latter half of the twentieth century there occurred a considerable amount of political *de*consolidation: a substantial number of new independent nations have been created owing to the breakup of the Soviet Union and Yugoslavia, and to the dissolution of the great Western European colonial empires. Third, the hard fact remains that almost all the political consolidations that occurred in the past were brought about by warfare, and in the nuclear age, additional warfare offers an unattractive avenue toward further political consolidation leading to a world state. Finally, inasmuch as the question of inevitability is only sensibly considered with reference to existent reality, and as world government is not yet part of existent reality, the word "inevitable" is clearly an overstatement. Although it is apparent from the principle of causation either that a world state *will* be a part of the future history of human civilization, or that it *will not* be, we do not know which of these outcomes will actually occur.

Nevertheless, one need not take Wendt's "inevitability proposition" seriously to recognize that the contribution is significant. Thirty years ago, the publication of an article like "Why a World State Is Inevitable" in a reputable international relations periodical would have been virtually unimaginable. It seems unlikely that Professor Wendt firmly believes in a literal interpretation of the inevitability proposition. Rather his purpose was to stimulate interest in and discussion among his colleagues of a possibility that he believes *ought* to happen: namely the foundation of a world state. Wendt leaves open the question of the precise nature of the world state, and hints that it would probably be something less powerful and centralized than the omnipotent world state of orthodox world federalist thinking. Likely it would be a *limited* world government, as opposed to an *unlimited* world government (the omnipotent world state).

Limited World Government

In fact, the concept of limited world government has been coming into increasingly clear focus in recent sympathetic contributions on world government by authors such as Luis Cabrera, Louis Pojman, Torbjörn Tännsjö, Daniel Deudney, and James Yunker.[9] These contributions are working toward a fundamental reconstitution of the concept of state sovereignty to achieve a workable compromise between the realities of today's nationally oriented world, and the possibility of a more cosmopolitan world in the future. Important elements of the proposed compromise are exemplified by Yunker's proposal for a limited world government tentatively designated the "Federal Union of Democratic Nations." As this is the most detailed institutional blueprint for limited world government currently available in the published literature, for convenience it will be used in the following as an illustrative example of the concept.[10]

As the name implies, the Union would be a federal rather than a unitary form of government. This means that the member nations would maintain their separate identities, governments and cultures, and would retain substantial independence, autonomy and sovereignty in all matters that do not impinge heavily on the welfare of other member nations. No officials of existing national governments would be either appointed or approved by the supernational government; rather these officials would be elected or appointed by whatever means are already employed.

The tentative name of the federation also implies that the member nations would all be democratic in nature. A fairly generous interpretation of the term "democratic" may be necessary, lest too many nations be denied membership on the basis that they are not sufficiently democratic. In a general sense, "democracy" implies that the government is responsive to the preferences of the people. But more specifically, it implies that high government officials are elected by the citizens in regular, open, and contested elections (accountability of the leadership), and that the citizens enjoy strong and effective rights of free speech, free press, and free political organization.

A substantial number of nations in the world today—even some that proclaim themselves to be democratic—do not exhibit these characteristics. For example, the People's Republic of China is today regarded by many people as a political oligarchy under the effective control of a handful of high officials of the Communist Party of China. But it would be highly inadvisable to exclude a nation as important as China from the Federal Union on grounds that it is insufficiently democratic. If China were a member nation of the Federal Union of Democratic Nations, then there would be stronger and more effective psychological pressure on the leadership to implement democratic reforms, than there would be if China were not a member nation. The same is true of smaller nations that at the present time are not internally democratic in the strong sense.

The envisioned Federal Union would be a full-scale, functioning state far beyond the United Nations of today. It would possess the authority to impose taxes and maintain military forces. Its legislative, executive and judicial branches would be subject to ultimate democratic control via free elections. It would have a capital city and a permanent administrative apparatus, a flag, an anthem, emblems, and various other forms and trappings of state authority. On the other hand, there would be various limitations on its power and authority that are quite inconsistent with conventional notions of national sovereignty.

First and probably most fundamental of all, the federal world government would not possess a monopoly on large-scale armed force. Rather, each and every member nation of the world federation would retain a permanent and inalienable right to maintain independent control over whatever military personnel and armaments it deems necessary, including nuclear weapons. The Federal Union would directly control its own armed force, but it would not be an overwhelming armed force: perhaps something along the lines of contemporary Britain's military capability. This stipulation, of course, runs directly contrary to the traditional world federalist dream of a world instantly purged of the threat of nuclear world war. The problem with this dream is its utter impracticality: it is virtually impossible to conceive that the great powers would agree voluntarily to full disarmament within the foreseeable future. On the other hand, if the member nations of a world federation along the lines of the Federal Union are permitted to keep their military capabilities intact, there is a possibility that as the years and decades go by, greater mutual trust and respect will evolve among the nations participating in the world federation, enabling a gradual but steady reduction of their military commitments.

Closely allied to the retained national right to independent military forces would be the retained national right to free and unopposed secession from the world federation at any time at the unilateral discretion of the nation. This provision, along with the provision for independent national military forces, suggests that membership in the world federation would not be universal for a very long time, if ever. This is not necessarily a problem. Once membership becomes sufficiently widespread, strong "gravitational forces" would operate on the remaining nations to persuade most of them to join. This has been seen, for example, in the history of the European Union. The lure of joining a large and prosperous free trade area eventually brought the United Kingdom into the fold. Moreover, if indeed a small number of nations choose to remain permanently outside the world federation, most probably this would not constitute a significant impediment to its effectiveness.

Although a unicameral form is envisioned for the Federal Union legislature, some of the virtues of bicameralism would be captured by a proposed "dual voting system." Whenever a vote is taken in the federation legislature, the measure being considered would have to be approved by a majority on two different bases: the population basis and the material basis. In the population vote, the weight given to the vote of each particular representative would be proportional to the population of his/her district, relative to the total population of the Federal Union. In the material vote, the weight given to the vote of each particular representative would be proportional to the financial revenues derived from his/her district, relative to the total financial revenues of the Federal Union. Representatives from rich nations would be disproportionately represented in the material vote, while representatives from populous poor nations would be disproportionately represented in the population vote. Since measures would have to be approved on both the material basis and the population basis, only measures on which rich nations and poor nations could achieve a reasonable degree of consensus would have a chance of being approved by the federation legislature.

The dual voting system would prevent the passage of legislation aimed at a drastic redistribution of current world income (which would be opposed by the rich nations), and it would also prevent the passage of legislation that might be viewed as reestablishing conditions of colonial exploitation (which would be opposed by the poor nations). Skeptics might argue that the proposed dual voting system in the world legislature would inevitably result in a "gridlock" condition preventing the passage of any useful and effective world legislation. One might ask how the current international regime, based on the sovereign nation-state system, can possibly avoid analogous gridlock. At least with a functioning world government in existence, there would be a reasonable probability that more effective global action could be mobilized against global problems than is currently being mobilized.

Obviously the dual voting system is inconsistent with the traditional world federalist ideal of pure democracy, wherein each citizen of the polity exercises one and only one vote. This is a third major difference, along with free exit and independent national military forces, between the Federal Union proposal and the conventional world federalist proposal. In an ideal world in which all nations had comparable living standards, this departure from the one-person-one-vote principle would not be necessary. But it is important to recognize that the practical relevance of the distinction between the population vote and the material vote would be eliminated were all nations of the world to have approximately equal per capita income. Dual voting, and other institutional proposals designed to cope with the North-South economic gap, are intended as a short-run solution to the problem. The long-run solution would be to eliminate the gap.

A Global Marshall Plan

The idea of a Global Marshall Plan to eradicate, or at least greatly reduce, the problem of world poverty has long been a staple of visionary thinking, and dates back at least to the "world government boom" of the immediate post-World War II period.[11] From time to time, advocacies of the idea have appeared in mainstream venues. For example, George J. Church published an editorial entitled "The Case for a Global Marshall Plan" in the June 12, 1978, issue of *Time Magazine*. Over the last several years, the idea has been vigorously advocated by the Global Marshall Plan Initiative, a pressure group mainly active in the European Union countries.

A Global Marshall Plan (GMP) would be a natural complement to a world federation, and were the latter to be established, the GMP would likely be a principal concern of the federation over the first several decades of its existence. At the present time, public opinion in the rich countries toward foreign aid can hardly be described as favorable. Self-reliance is a virtue, and most people in the rich nations today feel that it is the sole responsibility of the poor nations to provide their own capital resources through saving and investment. Unfortunately, world economic history up to the present time has generated a situation whereby it is unlikely that the economic gap will be appreciably narrowed within the foreseeable future, unless the rich nations convey very large amounts of investment resources to the poor nations. The special conditions which in the past led to dramatic economic progress in the rich nations (e.g., the opening up of the North American landmass to Western European colonization) no longer exist, nor will they ever again exist. The economic gap is likely to be virtually permanent unless the rich nations make a conscious policy decision to provide the productive resources to the poor nations necessary to close it.

The discipline of economics, as is the case with other social scientific disciplines that aspire to the pure scientific status associated with the hard sciences, prefers to study the world as it is (positive analysis) rather than the world as it should be (normative analysis). Since nothing like a global Marshall Plan has ever been attempted in the real world, evaluation of the possibility is virtually absent from the professional economic literature. However, it is not quite true to say that no scientific evidence at all exists that a Global Marshall Plan could be successful. To supplement the political proposal for a Federal Union of Democratic Nations, James A. Yunker, an economist by profession, has also put forward a complementary economic proposal for a GMP tentatively designated the World Economic Equalization Program (WEEP), and has done a significant amount of preliminary research to evaluate its potential effectiveness.[12]

The WEEP envisions a major expansion of existing foreign development assistance programs into a full-fledged GMP, whereby nations such as the United States, Japan, the Western European nations, and other wealthy nations, would contribute in the range from two to four percent of their Gross National Products to a transfer fund for the purpose of increasing the "generalized capital" stocks of the recipient nations (this category encompasses business physical capital, human capital, and social overhead capital). These contributions would be much greater than existing contributions, but may be within the range of political feasibility, since military expenditures currently account for larger percentages of GNP, especially for the superpowers.

Employing computer simulations of a model of the international economy, the research shows the possibility of a dramatic narrowing of the economic gap within a 50-year planning period, at the relatively minor cost to the donor nations of a very small decrease in the rate of rise of their per capita incomes. Obviously computer simulations are not necessarily a reliable guide to reality, and in fact Yunker presents results from alternative simulations, using pessimistic assumptions, that show the possibility that the GMP would fail. His position is that the GMP should be undertaken on a tentative and provisional basis, with the understanding that if after a reasonable trial period between 10 and 20 years, the program is not making significant progress in narrowing the economic gap, then it will be gradually downsized and eventually terminated. Since it cannot be reliably determined, on the basis of presently existing knowledge, whether or not a Global Marshall Plan would be successful, the only way to answer this question in a truly objective and scientific manner is to apply the experimental method: to initiate the program and observe the outcome.

Clearly, this trial-and-error approach also applies to the Federal Union itself. If it is established, and afterward fails to make a positive contribution to global governance, then the open door policy allows for its peaceful dissolution. The fact that an "exit strategy" is available if needed significantly reduces the risk involved in such an undertaking. At the same time, if the initiative is successful, powerful institutional support will have been created toward gradual improvement in the processes of global governance, and the assurance of long-term human destiny. In light of the large upside benefit, the modest downside risk might be deemed acceptable.

Hegemony versus Guidance

As the third millennium gets underway, the human prospect is both promising and perilous. International trade and investment have advanced to the point where the term "world economy" is no longer an exaggeration but rather established fact. Technological progress has brought about economic living standards for a substantial proportion of the world's human population that would have been unimaginable in earlier times. People at opposite ends of the world can communicate instantaneously with each other, and are physically separated by no more than a few hours of travel via jet aircraft. Although religious and ideological distinctions still abound, a reasonable degree of consensus has been reached among informed people around the world on some key components of proper individual behavior and social organization.

But while economic, technological and cultural globalization have knitted the world together as never before, political globalization is at a virtual standstill. Although the imperfections and weaknesses of the United Nations are widely acknowledged, no proposals are being given serious consideration for establishing a supernational organization qualitatively beyond the U.N. Meanwhile, the surface area of the Earth continues to be subdivided among a little over 200 jealously independent and self-righteously sovereign nation-states. Virtually every nation, large and small, feels that it must necessarily support a substantial military capability to avoid humiliation or despoliation at the hands of other nations. Now that military technology has produced thermonuclear weapons and intercontinental ballistic missiles—weapons which every superpower deems essential to its national security, continuation of time-honored, nineteenth-century, balance-of-power modes of thinking about international relations and foreign policy is fraught with peril.

Approximately 100 years ago, a sense of smug complacency had settled over the world. Even though the major Western European nations were deeply enmeshed in an arms competition, the consensus was that no major war would occur because there was no need for one. After all, the European superpowers of the era were all signatories to the agreements of the Hague peace conferences of 1899 and 1907, among which was the "Convention for the Pacific Settlement of International Disputes." Quoting from this Convention: "In case of serious disagreement or conflict, before an appeal to arms, the Signatory Powers agree to have recourse, as far as circumstances allow, to the good offices or mediation of one or more friendly powers." Moreover, the Permanent Court of Arbitration had been established to deal with any and all international disputes. Unfortunately, these good intentions were completely overthrown by a single terrorist act: the assassination by a teenaged Serbian nationalist by the name of Gavrilo Princip of the Austrian archduke and his wife in Sarajevo on June 28, 1914. The fraught circumstances following the assassination did not allow "recourse to the good offices or mediation of one or more friendly powers." And thus was initiated the terrific cycle of violence from 1914 through 1945 known as World Wars I and II.

In light of the terrible events of September 11, 2001, it cannot be doubted that there are nihilistic terrorist groups in the world today fully analogous to the Black Hand conspirators behind Gavrilo Princip. These groups dream of the day when they can improve on the 9/11 success of Al Qaeda by detonating a nuclear bomb within a major First World city, most likely in the United States. In 1914, the great powers of the day were drawn into conflict by disagreement over how far an injured nation could go to suppress terrorist organizations operating outside its national boundaries. A truly catastrophic terrorist attack in the future might reproduce the conditions of 1914. The possibility of terrorist attacks is heightened to the extent that there are "pressures" of various kinds in the world, The contemporary combination of increasing global economic inequality, mushrooming population, and environmental deterioration is likely to be richly productive of "pressures" into the foreseeable future.

It is axiomatic among informed Americans today that there can be no going back to the isolationism of earlier times. Economic, technological and cultural globalization has proceeded to the point that it is no longer possible for the United States of America to turn its back on the rest of the world—to let the rest of the world "take care of itself," so to speak. It is assumed by virtually all analysts that if the U.S. were to do anything like that, adverse developments would soon occur throughout the world that would eventually constitute a dire threat to U.S. national interests. That U.S. foreign policy must necessarily be internationalist can no longer be seriously questioned. But exactly what sort of internationalist policy is most advisable? A rich literature continues to address this question.[12]

Unfortunately, this rich literature virtually ignores the possibility of world government. It is agreed among the analysts that although the United States is currently the single most powerful nation in the world in terms of economic output and military capability, it does not have sufficient resources on its own to establish and maintain a global hegemony. A cooperative relationship must be established with other nations. The basic question debated by policy analysts is—on the assumption of continuation of the contemporary system of fully sovereign and independent nations—how much sacrifice of short-term U.S. national interests should be undertaken in order to benefit long-term U.S. national interests. But no matter what the United States does, its policies tend to interpreted by some nations as narrowly self-interested grabs for more power and domination.

A superior tradeoff between short-term and long-term national interests would probably be achieved—for the United States as well as for all other nations—if all or most of the world's nations were united in a limited, but fully functional, federal world government along the lines described in the foregoing. Such a government obviously would not mark the "end of history," in the sense of immediately and definitively solving the world's problems. Rather it would be an organic part of history, that would provide a firmer institutional foundation for the further evolution of effective global governance, and foster an international atmosphere in which U.S. policies would be perceived as benign efforts at guidance toward universally beneficial outcomes.

Notes

1. Lloyd E. Ambrosius, *Woodrow Wilson and the American Diplomatic Tradition; The Treaty Fight in Perspective* (Cambridge: Cambridge University Press, 1990); John Milton Cooper, *Breaking the Heart of the World: Woodrow Wilson and the Fight for the League of Nations* (Cambridge: Cambridge University Press, 2010); J. Michael Hogan, *Woodrow Wilson's Western Tour: Rhetoric,*

Public Opinion, and the League of Nations (College Station, Tex.: Texas A&M University Press, 2006).

2. Townsend Hoopes and Douglas Brinkley, *FDR and the Creation of the U.N.* (New Haven, Conn.: Yale University Press, 2000); Stephen C. Schlesinger, *Act of Creation: The Founding of the United Nations* (New York: Basic Books, 2003); Justus D. Doenecke and Mark A. Stoler, *Debating Franklin D. Roosevelt's Foreign Policies, 1933-1945* (Lanham, Md.: Rowman & Littlefield, 2005).

3. A detailed account of the postwar world government boom is presented in Joseph P. Baratta, *The Politics of World Federation, Vol. I: United Nations, UN Reform, Atomic Control, Vol. II: From World Federalism to Global Governance* (Westport, Conn.: Praeger, 2004).

4. Emery Reves, *The Anatomy of Peace* (New York: Harper, 1945); Dexter Masters and Katherine Way, editors, *One World or None: A Report to the Public on the Full Meaning of the Atomic Bomb* (New York: McGraw-Hill, 1945); Frederick L. Schuman, *The Commonwealth of Man: An Inquiry into Power Politics and World Government* (New York: Alfred A. Knopf, 1952).

5. See Derek Heater, *World Citizenship and Government: Cosmopolitan Ideas in the History of Western Political Thought* (New York: St. Martin's Press, 1996), for an account of the development of the idea of world government in intellectual history from the time of Alexander the Great to the early 1990s.

6. Émeric Crucé, *The New Cyneas* (originally published in French in1623). Edited with an English translation by Thomas W. Balch under the title *The New Cyneas of Émeric Crucé* (Philadelphia: Allan, Lane and Scott, 1909). Reprinted by Kessinger Publishing, 2010. Immanuel Kant, *Perpetual Peace: A Philosophical Essay* (originally published in German in 1795). Translated with an introduction by Mary Campbell Smith (London: Swan Sonnenschein & Co., 1903). Reprinted by Cosimo Classics, 2005.

7. Kenneth H. Waltz, *Man, the State and War: A Theoretical Analysis* (New York: Columbia University Press, 1959), p. 228.

8. Alexander Wendt, "Why a World State Is Inevitable," *European Journal of International Relations* 9(4), October 2003, pp. 491-542.

9. Luis Cabrera, *Political Theory of Global Justice: A Cosmopolitan Case for the World State* (New York: Routledge, 2004); Louis P. Pojman, *Terrorism, Human Rights, and the Case for World Government* (Lanham, Md.: Rowman & Littlefield, 2006); Daniel Deudney, *Bounding Power: Republican Security Theory from the Polis to the Global Village* (Princeton, N.J.: Princeton University Press, 2007); Torbjörn Tännsjö, *Global Democracy: The Case for a World Government* (Edinburgh: Edinburgh University Press, 2008); James A. Yunker, *The Grand Convergence: Economic and Political Aspects of Human Progress* (New York: Palgrave Macmillan, 2010).

10. The most extended treatment of the "blueprint specifics" of the Federal Union proposal is contained in Chapter 2 ("A Pragmatic Blueprint for World

Government") of James A. Yunker, *Political Globalization: A New Vision of Federal World Government* (Lanham, Md.: University Press of America, 2007).

11. Although world federalists in the post-World War II era have viewed a world government primarily as an instrument for the reduction of the risk of a nuclear war among the superpowers, they have also viewed such a government as an instrument through which to overcome the long-term threat to international harmony and permanent peace represented by the economic gap between rich nations and poor nations. One of the earliest expressions of this particular vision was contributed by the historian Stringfellow Barr, a member of the "Committee to Frame a World Constitution" formed by Robert Hutchins and Giuseppe Borgese of the University of Chicago in the immediate aftermath of the Second World War. In 1950, following completion of the Committee's work and the publication of their "Preliminary Draft of a World Constitution," the University of Chicago Press published a 30-page pamphlet by Barr entitled "Let's Join the Human Race." The themes and ideas in this short tract were later amplified in his book *Citizens of the World* (New York: Doubleday, 1952), which boasted a preface by Justice William O. Douglas of the U.S. Supreme Court. Barr asserted that the interdependent goals of world government and worldwide economic equalization should be pursued simultaneously, since neither one was likely to be achieved in the absence of the other.

12. James A. Yunker, *Common Progress: The Case for a World Economic Equalization Program* (New York: Praeger, 2000). A somewhat revised and updated version of the research reported in the book is contained in James A. Yunker, "Could a Global Marshall Plan Be Successful? An Investigation using the WEEP Simulation Model," *World Development*, 32(7), July 2004, pp. 1109-1137.

13. Michael Mandelbaum, The Case for Goliath: *How America Acts as the World's Government in the 21st Century* (New York: Public Affairs Press, 2005); Leslie Gelb, *Power Rules: How Common Sense Can Rescue American Foreign Policy* (New York: HarperCollins, 2009); David E. Sanger, *The Inheritance: The World Obama Confronts and the Challenges to American Power* (New York: Harmony Books, 2009); David Held and Mathias Koenig-Archibugi, editors, *American Power in the 21st Century* (Malden, Mass.: Polity Press, 2004); Zbigniew Brzezinski, *The Choice: Global Domination or Global Leadership* (New York: Basic Books, 2004); Amitai Etzioni, *From Empire to Community: A New Approach to International Relations* (New York: Palgrave Macmillan, 2004); Strobe Talbott, The *Great Experiment: The Story of Ancient Empires, Modern States, and the Quest for a Global Nation* (New York: Simon and Schuster, 2008); Fareed Zakaria, *The Post-American World* (New York: W. W. Norton, 2008).

Index

About the Author

James A. Yunker was educated at Fordham University (B.A., 1965), the University of California at Berkeley (M.A., 1966), and Northwestern University (Ph.D., 1971). He is Professor of Economics at Western Illinois University (Macomb, Illinois), where his teaching responsibilities include microeconomic theory, mathematical economics, and econometrics. Yunker has published numerous articles in professional journals and several books. His most recent books include *The Idea of World Government: From Ancient Times to the Twenty-First Century* (2011), *The Grand Convergence: Economic and Political Aspects of Human Progress* (2010), and *Political Globalization: A New Vision of Federal World Government* (2007). Yunker's special interest has been the application of economic methodologies to diverse real-world problems and issues ranging from the performance evaluation of college and university faculty to the potential effectiveness of capital punishment as a deterrent to homicide. An important component of Yunker's research and writing deals with visionary projects in the areas of socio-economic organization (pragmatic market socialism), foreign development assistance (a Global Marshall Plan), and world government in the form of a supernational federation tentatively designated the Federal Union of Democratic Nations.